The SECURE SOUL

FINDING INNER STRENGTH AND CONNECTION WHEN TRUST DOESN'T COME EASY

DR. ALISON COOK

W Publishing Group
An Imprint of Thomas Nelson

The Secure Soul

Published in Nashville, Tennessee, by W Publishing, an imprint of Thomas Nelson. W Publishing and Thomas Nelson are registered trademarks of HarperCollins Christian Publishing, Inc.

The author is represented by Alive Literary Agency, www.aliveliterary.com.

ISBN 978-1-4003-5262-3 (audiobook)
ISBN 978-1-4003-5261-6 (eBook)
ISBN 978-1-4003-5260-9 (TP)

Library of Congress Control Number: 2026936096

Printed in the United States of America

26 27 28 29 30 LBC 5 4 3 2 1

For every tender soul
who is learning to trust again.

CONTENTS

PART ONE

HOW TRUST BREAKS

CHAPTER 1

THE ACHE OF DISCONNECTION

A part of me doesn't like God very much.

I discover this surprising truth on a late-night prayer walk.

I am on a trip with my husband in London. His work has brought him here, and he asked if I wanted to join him. I almost didn't go, protesting that I had too much work to do, even though our kids are fully launched, out of our home, and my own work can be done from anywhere, including from London. But thankfully, despite my inner resistance, I am here.

As he usually does, he has invited me to come along for his late-night prayer walk. Typically, back home when this invitation comes, I think, *I should do that sometime*, as I sink into my warm bed or into whatever show I'm watching.

Tonight is different. We are in London. It seems insane not to take him up on the offer to walk through the dark night under the electric, pulsing lights of Regent Street, an iconic stretch of modern bustle and old-world sophistication. Though the shops are mostly closed by 10:00 p.m., the time of our late-night prayer walk, their window displays still sparkle like invitations. People spill out of late-night pubs and cozy restaurants, their laughter rising above the hum of traffic.

I feel giddy as we head out of our hotel and turn right past a giant Gothic church, its pointed arches and old stained-glass windows lit up in red and yellow. I am aware that my husband is trying to pray, but I cannot stop myself from tugging at his arm, like a child, trying to get him to see what I see. He laughs and plays along. We start a game of "Quaker Meeting," to see who can hold on to the silence. I keep breaking, so we turn around, walk back across the street to the entrance of our hotel, and start the walk over. This is just the kind of banter that I love sharing with him.

After a few back-and-forths, I finally surrender. We each sink into the silence of our own thoughts as we walk side by side deeper into the city lights.

This is a prayer walk, I think. *I really should pray.*

But a part of me doesn't want to. And that's when I notice this feeling inside me—a very distinct feeling of *I don't like God very much.*

I connected to a younger part of myself earlier in the week, a young girl inside who was over the moon with joy to be seeing the sights of London.

I'm not surprised she's tugging at the corners of my soul again tonight. She senses she has my attention for the first time in a long while.

It's she who doesn't want to pray, I realize. She's the one who was playfully trying to distract my husband. She's here with me now and wants nothing to do with God . . . or anything that smacks of religiosity, for that matter.

I try to reason with her, not using words, but sending her ideas.

What if I pray with my eyes open, as we share with God what we are seeing? I think, trying to get her to buy into my we-really-should-be-praying agenda.

I don't want to, she doubles down.

I'm confused. I don't get it. Ninety percent of me is quite fond of God and enjoys talking with him. But tonight, this young part of me is stubbornly insistent.

I decide to get curious about her, a tactic I have helped others practice for decades.

Okay. We don't have to pray. But while we walk, can I try to understand why you don't like God very much?

It's the same sort of negotiation I've learned to use as a parent of my real-life kids. Here's the deal: I'll do whatever you want on this outing. The only catch is that you have to talk to me.

He's no fun! That's the first thing I sense from her, this young one inside me who jumps at the chance to be heard. What follows is a cascade of images and impressions: stiff church clothes, overly wrought religious discussions, warnings not to giggle too much. In her world, God is more like a strict school principal than a wonder-seeking playmate. He feels distant and serious. Definitely not someone who shares in her current state of playfulness.

I feel in my body what she feels but can't quite express. It's a sort of tense, moralistic dogmatism that every cell in my body rejects. She is alive with curiosity and delight. It's no wonder she doesn't want to connect with this God who—in her mind—is a buzzkill, more concerned with rules than relationship, more interested in compliance than connection, more focused on her performance than her delight. She wants to dance, to explore, to feel *alive* in this moment.

I'm tempted to talk her out of these feelings, to quote Bible verses about what God is really like, the God most of me has experienced.

What about Jesus? I try to reason with her. *He loves the little children.*

She's not biting. More images flash through my mind. Jesus with drapey robes and long cocker-spaniel hair speaking in lofty, hard-to-understand words. It's as if he's a caricature in my mind of every bad drawing or cliché-ridden book or movie, coming in to shut down any semblance of wonder, humor, or joy. She is not interested in this religious, morally pious version of God. Not one bit.

I want to laugh at her imagery. It's vivid. I understand what she means.

I also kind of want to cry. I want her to know that these caricatures she's internalized *are not God*. That they may have taken root in fear or been shaped by human distortion, but they are not reflective of the One whose presence fills the universe yet who still draws close to every single tender heart. The God of spacious places, of quiet joy, and of deep, loving attentiveness.

But I recognize that reasoning with her is not what she needs.

She is responding to my *presence*, to my being *with* her. So I continue to attune to her.

If you start to pray, you'll leave me.

I am taken aback by this more vulnerable feeling I sense from her.

I flash to a memory of an early encounter with my stepchildren, back when love was still finding its way. Their mom had passed away when they were very young, and I had just started dating their dad. Early on, they would physically wriggle their bodies in between their dad and me. They didn't mind my presence, as long as it was clear that I would not come between their bond with him.

The young one inside me is now telling me something through this memory, through identifying with the experience of my stepkids.

You mean you see God as a threat to your bond with me?

I sense an inner shrug from her, a sort of, *I can't help how I feel.*

I am not sure what to do with this new information.

Why would she see God as a threatening stepparent?

I turn my attention to God for a moment, who is also there with me, though this young one doesn't yet know it. "What do you make of this?" I ask with wide eyes.

Stay with her, God says. *She needs you.*

ATTACHMENT, REIMAGINED

I think what I'm really trying to tell you through this story is that I have attachment issues.

I feel anxious about connecting with others, and sometimes I feel anxious about connecting with God. On one hand, I worry I'll be consumed, overwhelmed, or even annihilated by other people . . . or by God. On the other hand, I fear being rejected, ignored, or alone. It's quite the inner conundrum.

I'll admit, I don't love the word *attachment*, even though as a therapist, I know how essential it is to our emotional and relational well-being. It sounds so cold, so clinical, like a distant clinician scribbling notes and diagnosing, "Patient has *attachment* issues."

But I do.

We all do, really.

Some of us more than others.

And it is precisely because so many of us wrestle with ongoing feelings of being un-*attached*—unseen by others, distant from intimacy, untrusting, or even isolated—that I tend to prefer a broader term to describe this foundational human need: *connectedness*.

Because at its core, attachment is just a more specific name for our deepest, most primal need for *connection*.

Our need for presence.

Our need to be held.

Our need to know we are not alone.

In short, our need for *love*.

We are born into the world reaching for connection.

Before we ever form words or beliefs, something in us longs to be seen, soothed, and safe.[1] Long before language or understanding, love is first learned through the body, through the gaze of a parent, the rhythm of a heartbeat, or the gentle tone that tells us, *You belong here.*

In psychology this is known as *attachment*—the deep, invisible bond that first forms between a child and their parent. It's the first experience of connectedness that shapes the way we come to trust and feel secure.

Will someone come when I cry?

Is love steady or unpredictable?

Do I matter enough to be noticed?

These questions are answered long before we can speak them.

If your caregivers consistently responded to your needs, you likely internalized a steady message: *I can count on someone to show up for me*. That kind of steady attunement creates an inner base of safety. As an adult, it supports your ability to trust others, take healthy risks, and recover more quickly when life knocks you down. Psychologists call this "secure attachment."[2]

But if those early bonds were unsafe or unpredictable, you may struggle to feel secure. For example, you might brace for rejection, question if it's safe to depend on others, or feel isolated even in the middle of a crowd. This is the heart of attachment theory.[3]

There are many profound insights about human nature birthed out of attachment theory, including important breakthroughs about the role of parenting in early childhood development, and how early experiences of care and attunement shape the nervous system, the developing brain, and our lifelong relational instincts. Parents matter deeply. Early relationships matter deeply. None of that is in question.

But when attachment is treated as something that begins and ends with human bonds, something essential is lost. Human relationships become the source, the solution, and the burden-bearers of our deepest need for safety and belonging. And they simply cannot carry that weight.

That's where this book comes in.

The truth I want us to discover together is this: The deepest kind of secure attachment doesn't originate with parents. It isn't sustained only by family, friends, or partners. As vital as those relationships are, no human bond, no matter how loving, was ever meant to carry the full weight of our need to belong.

Secure attachment begins in the heart of God. It flows through imperfect human bonds, shaping our souls in real and embodied ways. And it always calls us back to its Source, back to the One who made us to live securely held in Love, even when human love falls short.

SECURE ATTACHMENT BEGINS IN THE HEART OF GOD.

This kind of security, at its deepest level, isn't something we get lucky with or miss out on if we're unlucky. It's not a prize reserved for those who had perfect parents or flawless relationships. Secure attachment is the imprint of Love itself, written into the design of every soul.

And the rediscovery of that Love—the journey back to that secure base—begins *inside* of us.

THE SPIRITUAL ROOTS OF ATTACHMENT

We learn to trust, or not to trust, within broader relational systems, networks of emotional exchange that shape us long before we have language for them. But those systems don't stay outside of us. We internalize them. They shape how we relate to our own hearts.

The same dynamics of fear and safety, pursuit and withdrawal, need and shame, don't just get played out between you and other people. They echo within your *own inner world,* carrying the imprint of the relationships that first taught you what love felt like.

You carry those patterns like root systems in the soil of your soul.

Over time, you don't just remember them.

You live from them.

Which means healing isn't only about repairing relationships with others. It's about restoring your *inner* capacity for connection. It's about tending your inner landscape where attachment now lives.

When you begin to notice, care for, and gently nourish that *inner* ecosystem, something sacred begins to take shape. What once felt fragmented or guarded starts to feel *tended.* Your inner being no longer feels abandoned.

And it is often there, in that place, that you begin to sense something else: *that a Presence has been with you all along.*

You start to experience God not only beyond you or above you, but *with you*, meeting you in the places where you once felt most alone. And from that shared presence, a deeper sense of *inner security* begins to form—one that no longer rises or falls on what others do or don't give.

From that growing security, you begin to notice:

- A sense of safety within yourself, because you are no longer alone inside.
- A secure base from which to connect with others, without losing yourself.
- A deeper, abiding sense of connectedness with a God who no longer feels distant, but near.

In psychology, attachment theory gave us a language for the ache of disconnection. But it rarely names the inner system: the *internalized voices* that play out in our external relationships.[4] And it almost never names the Source of attachment—the consistent presence of Divine Love, always drawing us back toward connection.

In this book, we'll explore the often-overlooked terrain of *inner attachment*: the disconnection you feel not only in your relationships with others but also within parts of your own soul.[5] The spiritual loneliness that runs beneath the surface of modern life, shaping how you relate, how you withdraw, how you long to be seen.

We'll also explore how God meets you in those innermost places, as the steady, loving Presence who has been with you all along, patiently restoring what disconnection has undone and threading every fragment back together. And as you tend that inner ecosystem, you'll begin to move more securely within your external networks of belonging, cultivating relationships that are vibrant and alive, tender and imperfect, shaped by both rupture and repair.

Because the ache of disconnection isn't only about feeling unseen by a parent, distant from a partner, or excluded by a friend. It's not just a byproduct of busy lives or too many notifications.

It runs deeper.

It's a *spiritual ache*—a longing for the Source of Love that holds us all together.[6] That love isn't something we create; it's something *we're invited to remember.* A Love that is the animating force of relationship itself, making human connection possible—not through outer perfection, but through *inner presence.*

This is the Love that has been with us from the beginning, woven through our earliest bonds, planted in the soil of our inner world, and alive in the space between us.

The One who reminds us: *You were never meant to do this life alone.*

The One who makes the garden grow both within us and among us.[7]

I want to reimagine secure attachment with you in the pages of this book—not as a label rooted in the distant past, but as a living force, a current of Love moving through every relationship, every silence, every ordinary moment.

THE FLOW OF CONNECTION

Still in London, I'm making my way through the bustling, crowded street, just trying to find a sandwich. I'm out by myself this time. Accustomed to rural spaciousness, I feel . . . untethered, like a signal that's lost its tower, bouncing around with nowhere to land. Only I'm not floating through airwaves; I'm moving through a chaotic sidewalk, dodging strangers and noise, trying not to lose my bearings. I can feel myself start to unravel.

Just get a sandwich, I whisper to myself. *Just focus.*

I will myself into a tiny market jam-packed with people, grab a sandwich and some apples, and get in line. I forget to pick up a basket, of course, because I'm hurrying, so I fumble the fruit I am carrying. One apple drops, then another. I frantically chase after them.

At the register, I can't figure out the card reader. Should I tap? Insert? Swipe? The machine is buzzing at me. So is my nervous system. Shoulders tight. Mind racing. I am getting frantic.

And then . . .

I sense a presence.

I look up.

A woman behind the cash register. Her large, kind brown eyes meet mine.

"It's okay," she says gently.

"Just insert the card here, like this. Here's a bag for your apples."

I feel tears rise. My body softens. I exhale.

Her presence anchors me. Her kindness tethers me.

I remember how to use the credit card machine. I am in my body again.

I am not alone in this urban galaxy of strangers. Someone

has *seen* me. I walk out of the market not just holding a sandwich, but held by *connection*.

And while this may seem like an incredibly unremarkable moment on the surface, it reveals a simple but profound truth about the flow of connection.

Somehow this woman felt something inside her that recognized something inside me. Maybe she'd felt anxious before. Maybe she'd been overwhelmed. I have no idea. But what I do know is that something in her sensed something in me. The kindness of her tone didn't arise out of a vacant soul. *It arose out of a soul that knew compassion.*

And because I was in touch with myself and aware of my own anxiety and disconnection, I didn't shut her compassion out. I let it in.

She extended a gift, a lifeline of connectedness, to me. And I was able to *receive* it.

Twenty years earlier, I would not have been able to receive the kindness of a stranger.

Different city, same chaos. A hardworking graduate student, neck-deep in an anxiety I didn't know how to face, I was late for a simple haircut and running on adrenaline. My body was rigid, my heart pounding so hard I could almost hear it as I raced into the salon, tipping over a magazine rack.

A stylist bent down to help me pick them up. "It's okay," she said. "You're good."

But I could not take her kindness in. I was cut off from myself, my body locked in urgency. And that woman's kindness bounced right off the inner wall I didn't even know I'd built. For the next hour I sat surrounded by the familiar buzz of dryers and the low hum of chatter. But inside, I stayed tense. At the front desk afterward, she tried again. "Are you okay?" she asked, her voice kind. I smiled tightly, shoved my payment into her hand, and bolted for the door—mortified, ashamed, and blaming myself.

I couldn't connect with myself. And because of that, I couldn't *receive* the lifeline she was throwing out to me.

When we aren't connected with the hurting or anxious or distant-from-God parts of ourselves, we can't receive the healing kindness of connection even when it is clearly extended to us. It's a painful dynamic, one I've lived from the inside out.

And once you've seen it in yourself, you start to notice it in others.

Have you ever tried to give someone a sincere compliment, and they simply refuse to take it? Or you genuinely tried to extend a kind word or a helping hand, and the other person stiffened up and rejected it, despite their clear need? No matter what you say, they find some way to deflect, downplay, or dismiss it. Every attempt at connection is shut down.

It's really hard to receive care from someone else if you're not in touch with your own inner ache—your own need for care, for kindness, for *connection*. And it's even harder to truly *care* for another person if you haven't learned to recognize your own inner disconnection first.

The first movement toward connectedness starts as you recognize the parts of *yourself* that long to be seen, known, and drawn back into relationship.

WHEN YOUR SOUL REACHES OUT

The truth is, something deeper was happening on that late-night prayer walk in London. A young part of my soul was reaching out. It wasn't just that this part of me didn't want to pray. It was that she wanted something she hadn't yet learned to associate with God.

She wanted closeness. Companionship. *To be with someone.*

What she needed wasn't more explanation, but a new way to connect.

There was a distance. A loneliness. A spiritual *dis*-connectedness that she had carried for years. And I hadn't known how to bridge it.

But that day, something shifted.

Instead of pushing that feeling away, I let myself turn toward the ache. I attuned to the shadowy place in my soul, without judgment and without trying to fix her. In doing so, I offered this part of myself a *lifeline of connection*—the same way the woman behind the cash register offered me a lifeline when she gently handed me the bag for my apples.

And something in me let this lifeline in.

I stayed present to this young place within me, instead of abandoning her. And she received that presence.[8] Paradoxically, this was the first step *toward* connection.

This young one didn't need correction or fixing or a sermon.

She needed *presence*.

She needed me to be *with* her.

To stay *near* her pain.

To hear her story of disconnection.

In that moment of attunement, space was made. Space for healing presence.

And here's what I've come to trust: The healing balm of presence is *so much* nearer than you think. It arrives the very moment you name the truth: *I'm disconnected.*

When do you feel it most?

Untethered. Alone. Distant.

Unseen. Unknown. Or simply overlooked.

It might be in your marriage.

In friendships.

With your children.

At work or in your neighborhood.

It might surface when you're by yourself, or when you try to reach for God.

Maybe there's been a rupture, a rejection, or a betrayal. Or maybe it's subtler than that. Maybe you've noticed a faint sense of distance, a loneliness that lingers even when you're not alone.

The truth is, we all feel disconnected at times. Renowned existential psychiatrist Irvin Yalom named isolation as one of the central struggles of being human. And while trauma or insecure attachment can intensify it, the core experience he described—the reality that no one can fully share or enter your inner world—is universal.[9] Even in the presence of others, there are places within that still feel alone.

THE HEALING BALM OF PRESENCE IS *SO MUCH* NEARER THAN YOU THINK.

Please hear me say: *Feeling alone or disconnected is not a sign that something is wrong with you.*

It's not a diagnosis. It's not a flaw.

It's an invitation.

A signal that you're alive, that you were made for connection.

It's your soul reaching out for love.

For closeness.

For safety.

And paradoxically, the path toward that connection is to first notice the isolated place within—the part of you carrying this ache.

It often sounds like this:

I feel alone. Even when I'm surrounded by other people.

I love my family, but sometimes I just want to run away.

I try to pray, but God feels distant.

I want love, but letting someone in feels risky.

Every time I open up, I end up hurt.

No one really knows me.

I know these voices well. I've longed for connection throughout my life—to feel close with others in a way that is mutual and safe and real. But the kind of intimacy where you let yourself be fully seen and trust the one who sees you has not come easily to me.

For a long time, I told myself I didn't need it. That the connections I saw around me weren't what they seemed. Shiny on the surface, but shallow, not necessarily more secure than my own company. Sometimes that was true. But it was never the whole story.

At other times, I'd tell myself there was something

wrong with *me*. That it was my fault I felt alone, even when surrounded by other people. That I was too much, not enough, or somehow wired incorrectly. That story wasn't any kinder.

My guess is you've told yourself similar stories. You've told yourself you don't really *need* the very connectedness you crave. Or you've blamed yourself for not being able to find it.

Neither of these messages is helpful . . . or true. Because beneath them both, something in us still knows that we were *always* meant for connection. But somewhere along the way, we stopped trusting it.

The question, then, is this: What exactly have we learned not to trust?

THE SACRED RHYTHM OF CONNECTION

Every moment you feel disconnected—when an argument erupts, loneliness creeps in, or distance grows—something tender happens beneath the surface. Your system pulls back. You brace. You tighten. Not because you're broken, but because you learned to protect what hurts.

And here's where we get trapped: We start asking human love to carry what it can't. We look to one relationship, or even one community, to hold the full weight of our need to be held and secure. And when it inevitably falters (because humans do), it can feel like *connection itself* isn't trustworthy.

It makes sense that you'd stop trusting, because your soul learned that reaching out can cost you. But the answer isn't to give up on people. And the answer isn't to shame yourself for needing them.

The invitation is deeper.

It's to return to *what makes connection possible in the first place:* to Love itself, steady as breath.

At its core, secure attachment isn't only psychological. It's *spiritual.* It's a sacred rhythm of connection sustained by God, the loving Presence who steadies us through both our breaking and our mending.

It's bigger than our own individual sense of safety. Bigger than any single relationship. Bigger than any one community.

It's the reality that we were made to move in rhythm with Love itself.

Every moment of life—whether you're standing in a supermarket line or walking down the streets of London; whether you're fighting with your spouse or frustrated with your children; whether you're alone or surrounded by friends—offers you a quiet invitation.

An invitation to return to Love. To reconnect.

This sacred rhythm of connection moves in two parts.

It starts when you *recognize* the moment you've shifted out of connection, whether you're anxious, overwhelmed, afraid, distant, or shut down.

Recognize: *I'm lonely.*

Recognize: *I've been hurt.*

Recognize: *I'm scared to trust.*

To *recognize* is:

- to notice
- to acknowledge something for what it truly is
- to remember something familiar
- to re-cognize—literally, "to know again"

And that moment of recognition is, in itself, a profound act of *re*-connection. It's the lifeline that pulls you back from your hurtling disconnection.

It's that quiet voice inside that says:

I see what's happening.

I know.

I'm aware.

It's the moment you tell the truth. And in that truth, you open the door.

From that open place, you can then *return*—to the sacred center within, to God's presence, to Love itself.

LIVING WITHIN THE SACRED RHYTHM OF CONNECTION MEANS LEARNING TO TRUST AGAIN AND AGAIN THE TRUTH OF THIS REALITY: *GOD ALREADY IS WHERE YOU ARE.*

Not to fix yourself or change someone else, but to return to what already *is*.

Return: *I am held, even in this painful moment.*

Return: *I am loved, even though I feel alone.*

Return: *I am known, in all of what I'm feeling.*

You've heard people say, "God meets you where you are." I'm saying something a little bit different:

God is already here.

Living within the sacred rhythm of connection means learning to trust again and again the truth of this reality: *God already is where you are.*

God never left.

Recognize: *the ache, the fear, the loneliness.*

Return: *to Love, the God who never left.*

This practice isn't a one-time fix. It's a rhythm you live into, like breath.

(Inhale) Recognize: *I'm disconnected.*

(Exhale) Return: *I am loved.*

(Inhale) Recognize: *I'm alone.*

(Exhale) Return: *God is already here.*

And when you practice this rhythm—again and again—you begin to experience connection in deeper and more lasting ways.

You begin to live into the rhythm of your design.

You stay connected within yourself.

You stay connected with other people, who love you, albeit imperfectly.

And above all, you stay connected with the God who is *always with you*, holding you, and them, and all the spaces in between.

This is what true connection feels like: returning . . . again and again . . . to Love.

THE SECURE SOUL

To cultivate what I call *the secure soul* is to practice this rhythm over and over: to *recognize* disconnection and *return*, again and again, to *Love*. From that inner place of safety, at the center of God's care, you learn to relate more honestly and wholeheartedly with others in a virtuous cycle of love.

This rhythm doesn't require perfection. It's not about fixing yourself, as if any of us could fix ourselves.

It only requires *presence*.

Each moment of fear, each pang of loneliness, each surge of anxiety, isn't failure, nor is it your destiny. Instead, it's an invitation to return to Love.

I recognize that I'm disconnected.

I return to Love.

Again and again: *Recognize. Return.*

Again and again: *Come home to Love.*

Here's the beautiful truth: You can *always* return to Love.

In the pages ahead, I'll share with you my own journey into the heart of Love—and how you can take that journey too. You'll hear how my attempts to control and criticize myself led to disconnection and chronic loneliness, and how I've learned to recognize those movements and return to Love instead.

THE SECURE SOUL IS NOT RESERVED FOR A FEW—IT'S THE CALLING OF EVERY HUMAN HEART.

And I'll help you recognize and understand these patterns of disconnection in your own life. Together, we'll make sense of these reactions and explore how to gently shift toward more connection.

The secure soul is not reserved for a few—it's the calling of every human heart. It's the journey of wholeness, of what Scripture calls *sozo*, the Greek word for healing.[10] It's the steady work of sacred transformation.

To build a secure soul is to create a sanctuary within your own self, an inner dwelling place where every part of your being is held in Love, a Love that flows from the inside *out*.

Are you ready to begin?

CHAPTER 2

THE PAIN OF NOT BEING CHOSEN

I'm at a massive women's conference, held at the largest church this Wyoming-raised, New England–shaped soul has ever stepped foot in. I've been invited to present a workshop, and I can't quite believe it. I've been planning my talk for months, along with my outfit.

I arrive at the large group gathering on the first night. I'm a cocktail of excitement and preparation, tinged with social anxiety. It's a familiar tension, yet somehow it still surprises me. It's that moment at every large group gathering or retreat when it feels like everyone else has already found their people while I'm standing there by myself, name tag clinging to my shirt, plastic cup in hand, scanning the room for an anchor.

No one is mean. That's not the issue. This is a women's

conference—in the South. Everyone is polite, well-mannered. Some smile; a few even say hello. But still, I'm on the outside. The other speakers seem to greet each other like old friends. They share jokes, easy hugs, and whispered updates between sessions. I hover at the edge of conversations I'm not part of, unsure where to step in. I'm trying to smile, even as something inside me begins to fade, quietly slipping beneath the surface.

As a large band begins to take the stage, I decide to find a seat. Trying to be inconspicuous, I slip into an aisle seat near the back, close to the door and out of everyone's way. But just as I begin to settle in, an usher gently taps my shoulder.

"Sorry," he says, "these seats are reserved for VIPs."

I'm mortified as I realize why the row was empty. The seats are roped off.

"I'm so sorry," I whisper, flustered. I don't want to walk all the way to the front—where the only open seats are—alone. Suddenly, my heels make me feel like I am a giraffe on stilts, and my bag feels enormous. I hate the feeling of being conspicuous. Of being seen in the wrong way.

So instead, I forego a seat altogether and decide to hover just outside the auditorium, near the entryway in the dark hall, pressing myself against the cold concrete wall, trying desperately to disappear.

My mind flashes back to college, those first days on my New England campus, thousands of miles from the small Wyoming town where I was born and raised. I arrived proudly sporting a brown plaid vest from Maurices, our local clothing store, and a freshly permed head of hair, bangs ratted up sky high. I had timed the perm perfectly for move-in day, blissfully unaware that no one in New England was getting perms . . . or wearing brown plaid vests. This was well before the internet stepped in to globalize local fashion trends.

I was on a freshman trip, a weekend of camping and hiking that was part of orientation before school began. Most of the large, chatty group came from Connecticut prep schools. I was the only student from one of those large rectangular flyover states out in the middle of nowhere.

I tried to blend in, edging into a nearby cluster of students, hoping no one would notice how out of place I felt. Until one guy turned and said, "Hey, watch it! You're on my sleeping bag!"

I apologized and quickly scampered away, humiliated that my attempt to include myself had been noticed—and rejected.

I don't belong here.

And now, decades later, at the women's conference, that same feeling washes over me. A completely different world, but the feeling is *exactly* the same:

I don't belong here.

It would take me years to connect the dots, but it was in moments like these, repeated over time, that this part of me, the one that doesn't like God very much, first took root: in the dark shadows where I convinced myself that the rejection I experienced was *my* fault. That if I had been different—less sensitive, less intense, less *me*—I might have been chosen. I might have belonged with the in-group.

THE ANCIENT ACHE OF ATTACHMENT

One of the most painful forms of disconnection is the pain of not being chosen. It's a specific kind of wound, one that reawakens older pain from childhood, from early friend groups, and even from how we've imagined God. You may have moved on from a painful season of not being chosen, but no matter how young or how old you were when it happened, your inner world doesn't always get the memo.

ONE OF THE MOST PAINFUL FORMS OF DISCONNECTION IS THE PAIN OF NOT BEING CHOSEN.

In my own life, no matter how many friendships I've built or how deeply I experience the love of my spouse or family, the moments of not being picked, of standing on the outside looking in, still linger. Like an old bruise on the psyche: mostly healed but tender when touched.

Maybe it's because I'm sensitive and wired to feel things deeply. Or maybe it's simply because I'm human. Because I'm pretty sure that this ache is universal.

We long to belong.

To be received.

To be met with *love*, *recognition*, and *welcome*.

To not only hear, but *feel* deep in our bones: *You're welcome here. Make yourself at home! You belong with us.*

Not lip service. Just a sense of authentic, deep *connectedness*.

Think about the last time you put yourself out there.

Maybe you invited a friend to something that mattered to you, left a voice memo that felt a little too honest, or hit "send" on a social media post that carried more truth than you usually share.

How many times did you check to see if there was a response?

What stirred in your chest as you waited?

What inner cringe did you feel?

Will I be received? Or will I be ignored?

Will I be welcomed in? Or will I be rejected?

You can tell yourself it's no big deal—that no one will notice your awkwardness, that you'll make a new friend, that it doesn't matter. But your soul doesn't quite believe you.

Beneath every instance of rejection—every unanswered message, every dismissive glance, every invitation withheld or crowded room where everyone seems to belong but you—there's a deeper story.

A story your body remembers.

A story your heart still holds.

A story with ancient roots.

Because these moments aren't just about now. They touch on old attachment wounds. They're about what's being *reactivated* in your nervous system, old imprints of disconnection from your earliest years, still tender beneath the surface.

Maybe it was the school dance where no one asked you to dance.

Or the time you were the last one picked for a team.

Or when your parent forgot to pick you up. Or when you needed comfort, and no one came.

Maybe it was when you raised your hand in class and

got laughed at, or when your best friend suddenly chose someone else.

These wounds don't only live in the past. They live in your body, shaping what you expect and how you interpret what's happening in the present. In vulnerable moments, they whisper an old message: *You don't belong here.*

And here's what's striking: The pain of not being chosen isn't just emotional. It's physical.

Neuroscience backs this up. Studies using brain imaging suggest that social rejection and exclusion light up some of the same neural networks involved in physical pain.[1]

When you are excluded, ignored, or dismissed, your brain registers it as a threat, like you've been punched.

The "punch to the gut" you feel in that moment of rejection isn't only metaphorical. It's neurological.

We are *wired* for connectedness—emotionally, neurologically, spiritually. To feel cherished by our families, embraced by our communities, and loved by God. This is our design. Which is why even small moments of rejection can feel so painful.

Our longing for connectedness is so primal that in moments of rupture, our whole system reacts. When connection breaks, our bodies tense, our minds race or shut down, and we grasp anxiously or retreat into avoidance.

All of these responses are signals: *Something vital feels lost.*

If you had a secure attachment base, you're better equipped to handle disconnection. If you didn't, those moments can shake you to your core. Regardless, every single one of us has to learn how to navigate it.

Because no matter what your childhood experience was like, we all experience moments of painful disconnection. Not making the team. Not getting the role. Not being chosen by the object of our affection. The social math of teenage years isn't kind: There is only one homecoming queen, one valedictorian, one sports star, one favorite. Most of us weren't it. And even the ones who were likely still had many moments of rejection.

And even as adults, it doesn't go away. We still face moments when we're not picked, not seen, not valued, not invited to the table.

The pain of not being chosen is a *universal wound*. One that lives deep inside many of us.

And how we recover . . . how we reconnect . . . how we grow through those moments . . . depends on the *inner resources* we can draw upon when the ache rises up again.

Because if we don't tend to ourselves in those moments—if we dismiss the ache, bury it, or try to spiritualize it away—the pain doesn't disappear. It burrows deeper.

It starts to echo through your sense of worth. It distorts your view of God. It clouds your capacity to feel loved at all. In this way, the pain of not being chosen becomes more than a relational rupture; it becomes a rupture within your soul.

SOUL RUPTURES

In psychology, we tend to think of a rupture as a disruption in the emotional bond between two people, a breakdown in connection that leaves one person feeling unseen, unsafe, or misunderstood. Sometimes it shows up in a heated argument. Other times, it's a sarcastic comment, a forgotten check-in, or a series of small interactions that accumulate over time. Whatever the form, something in the fabric of trust gets torn, and we feel it.

But the ruptures I worry about most aren't the ones that happen between two people. They're the ones that take root inside you, in the places in your soul that absorb what happens outside you. When those tender places go unattended, they begin to form an inner tear. I call this a *soul rupture*.

Whenever I see someone operating out of deep insecurity, fear, control, defensiveness, or even unhealed resentments (or when I notice these patterns in myself), the question I'm most interested in is this:

What happened inside that never got tended?

That's not to say other people don't contribute to your wounds. Of course they do. But what you can work with, and what ultimately shapes your healing, is what happens *within*.[2]

A soul rupture is a wound within your soul, whether big or small, that can be repaired through loving presence, tenderness, and honesty. But when you don't know how to tend to that inner wound, it doesn't stay small or isolated. What began as a moment of heartbreak or rejection—a wound that *could* have been a minor scratch or bruise—becomes something more entrenched.

Instead of healing, you reach for whatever gives you even a moment of relief. For most of us, that means doing what humans have done since the beginning of time: *You turn to shame or blame.*

You shame yourself.

- *I'm not good enough.*
- *Something must be wrong with me.*
- *I hate myself.*

You assume others have it figured out, and so of course, *you* must be the problem. You confuse not being chosen with proof that you're not worthy or good enough. You try to change yourself. You try to become more acceptable, more pleasing, less you.

Sometimes you blame others.

- *They're the problem!*
- *I don't need them.*
- *I can't stand them.*

You quietly sink into resentment, tearing others down in your mind while smiling on the outside. You judge others the way you fear you're being judged. You build walls to keep yourself safe.

And sometimes, you blame God.

- *Why would you let this happen?*
- *You must not care about me.*
- *Maybe you were never really there.*

You assume God has left you too. You think you've failed to earn God's blessing. Or you subtly start to pull away, concluding that God must be unfair, disappointed in you, or maybe not even there at all.

I've done all these things.

And here's the thing I need you to understand:

Neither shame nor blame closes the wound. They never have. They never will.

They don't mend the tear inside your soul. They don't repair the distance in your relationships. And they don't restore your connection with God.

NEITHER SHAME NOR BLAME CLOSES THE WOUND. THEY NEVER HAVE. THEY NEVER WILL.

When shame turns inward, telling you that you are the problem, or when blame hardens into contempt toward someone else, they don't close the rupture. They deepen it. They pull at the edges. They stretch the tear. What was a repairable rip becomes a deeper gash across the tapestry of your inner world.

That's why, when I felt that familiar ache of disconnection at the women's conference, I didn't shrug it off.

I knew all too well what happens when you don't pay attention. I'd walked the long road of shaming myself, resenting others, and sometimes blaming God. I'd felt the painful disconnection that shame and blame carve into the soul.

So this time, I chose something different. I didn't judge the ache or bury it. Instead, I followed it inward in order to tend the tear before it could become another gaping wound.

THE LONELIEST PLACE IN A CROWDED ROOM

Back at the women's conference, music soars from the main stage. Voices rise around me. People are singing, lifting their hands. I want to experience the feelings of connection others seem to be feeling, but I can't. Not at all.

I stand like a sentry at the edge of the auditorium, my giant bag held in front of me like a shield against some unseen ache. I mouth the words, trying to participate. But inwardly, I feel completely disconnected.

The fragmentation is building.

The soaring music. The crowded room. The invisible feeling of not quite belonging. In the past, I would have continued trying to fake it, hiding behind self-criticism or shame. But at this moment, I give myself the gift of a different path.

I recognize the ache. And I decide to reconnect: not to the group, but *to myself.*

I slip away from the crowd and find a blissful exit door to the giant stairwell. I climb up to the highest row of the auditorium balcony, the aching part of me desperate for something real.

Finally, I reach the top, where no one can see me. I am mercifully tucked behind the throngs of people all facing forward.

I sink to the floor with relief, setting down the giant bag I've been clutching. For the first time all evening, I let go of the weight of not being chosen, the weight of trying to pretend. I exhale.

Up here, in this lonely corner of the auditorium, I no longer feel alone.

It's here that I can finally begin to listen, not to the music still echoing below, but to the stirrings of my own soul.

And it's here, in the quiet, that I recognize her: a young,

teenage version of myself who has simply had *enough*. Down there, I felt invisible, fragmented.

But here, away from the noise, I can finally see a fuller picture of myself.

This younger version of me who has always felt so awkward, so out of her element, so on the outside looking in—she's not actually overly sensitive. She's not stupid or fragile or any of the dismissive labels I've silently assigned her to keep her at arm's length all these years. In fact, she's quite the opposite. She's more like a wild colt, untamed but passionate and fiery, longing for something real and ready to break free.

She may not be up for the polished performance happening down below. But she is fully alive, and aching for me to finally pay attention to her.

I can't find God here, she cries. *What's wrong with me?*

THE OUTSIDER WITHIN

In addition to being a therapist, I'm also trained as a psychologist of religion. My work has focused on how our experiences of God are shaped by our human relationships—how rejection, alienation, and wounding influence the way we connect (or struggle to connect) with the Divine.

Halfway through my doctoral training, I transferred out of a secular psychology program and into a joint program in psychology and theology because I couldn't bear to study the psyche, what I've always thought of as the soul, without also studying it in relation to God. I wanted a framework big enough to hold the whole person: body and spirit, nervous system and longing, attachment wounds and the search for meaning.

In the years since, I've grown wary of two extremes.

On one side is a version of psychology that treats the soul as a closed system, as if we could understand human wounding and longing apart from meaning, transcendence, and our intrinsic connection to others and to God.

On the other side is a version of faith that bypasses the soul altogether, as if we could connect with God while ignoring the very places inside us that are frightened, reactive, ashamed, hurting, or numb.

That's the lens I brought with me to the women's conference, and the one I bring to this book.

Because what was happening inside me that night wasn't only psychological. It was spiritual too. I felt painfully disconnected, not only from the group, but also from *God*. A part of me, one that had long felt like an outsider, was reemerging.

In that moment of disconnection, I felt that familiar ache of not fitting in, of not belonging. A soul rupture that tore right through all three relational dimensions:

- *What's wrong with me?*
- *What's wrong with them?*
- *What does this mean about God?*

Was it me—my social anxiety, my sensitivity to unspoken dynamics?

Was it them—an unspoken exclusivity I couldn't yet name?

Or was it something deeper still, a part of me surfacing with questions about God that still needed space to be heard?

I would come to find out that it was a mix of all these things. But in that moment, all I knew was this: *I was too fragmented to see clearly.* Before I could discern anything about the group or about God, I first needed to reconnect *within.*

Because beneath the swirl of anxiety, it was clear that the overwhelming ache was coming *from a specific place inside.* It was coming from a *part* of me who needed to tell her story.

A part of my soul who was still young, tender, and spiritually hungry. A part of me who had been carrying questions alone for years. Questions about belonging, about what it means to feel chosen, about whether God was big enough to hold even her. I hadn't known how to see her, let alone how to tend to the ache she carried deep inside.

But when I finally paused to *recognize* this *inner* rupture, something shifted. I realized it wasn't primarily the present circumstance that needed addressing. It was a young place within me carrying a plea from the deepest part of my soul: *Please don't overlook me again.*

Recognize: *I don't belong.*

Return: *I am loved, even here.*

CHAPTER 3

INNER BIDS FOR CONNECTION

Up in the lonely corner of the giant auditorium, I am sitting with this young teenage part of me. I stroke her metaphorical hair as we sit together. I know how she feels. It's not new. But I haven't always fully listened to her.

You can't find God here? I ask gently.

I wish I could. Everyone else is, she says. *But I can't.*

She's confused.

I don't want to talk her out of this feeling. She's had plenty of that already. But I do want to *sit with her in it*, to stay present and reflect on it together. So I ask if I can share some of the places I *have* encountered God, places that are far away from this particular women's conference.

She nods. *She trusts me.*

Images surface immediately.

I see the homeless shelter where my family and I hosted small group gatherings each week for years with the smell of stew simmering in the background, wafting through a cinder block room lined with orange plastic chairs. The raw, unpolished questions that rose up. How *real* it all felt.

Then the colorful books on my wooden shelves: Kierkegaard, Weil, and Hauerwas—teaching me that God can hold complexity. Lewis, L'Engle, and Frankl—opening doorways into imagination. And my beloved contemplatives—Henri Nouwen, Teresa of Ávila, John of the Cross—finding God not in grand performances, but in moments of tiny, quiet presence.

And then, unexpectedly, a Catholic cathedral in Boston where my husband and I would go with his ninety-year-old Lithuanian mother before she passed away. I see the man she called the "dancing priest," the way he would glide down the aisle and offer her the Eucharist in her wheelchair before anyone else. The way it lit up her face that she was *first*.

And how enchanted I felt, watching hundreds of people from all walks of life slowly make their way forward to receive bread, honor ancient words, and participate in something older and more global than anything I had experienced. A gathering that's been unfolding for centuries, long before modern American evangelicalism emerged.

I share these glimpses with her.

She is calmer now. She is *with* me.

Her body softens. Her confusion quiets. The loneliness lifts, just a little.

She still longs. But she doesn't feel so alone.

I continue to share with this tender, honest part of me all the ways we've connected with a big God.

A God expansive enough to hold *so many different kinds of* people across centuries.

A God who meets beloved children in homeless shelters and in cathedrals, in the wilderness and in crowded rooms, in prisons and in royal courts.

A God who welcomes prodigals, the brokenhearted, and who dignifies the ones the world forgets.

A God big enough to hold questions and mystery and raw ragged edges.

A God bigger than this moment. Bigger than this auditorium. An auditorium that suddenly feels small, less like a ginormous megachurch and more like a tiny, flickering room.

She's alert.

Listening.

Something in her begins to settle more deeply.

I like this God, I sense from her.

In my imagination I touch my lips to her hair. *I honor the bigness in you. I honor the bigness you seek.*[1]

I sit there in the balcony, next to the bag that had been my shield. Next to the heels I've removed from my feet.

The music pounds from the stage below.

Nothing has changed in the room.

But something has changed in me.

Not everything is healed. Not all the voices are quiet.

But something real has happened here:

I've begun to listen.

And the ache, finally, is being met.

She softens in my presence.

And I soften in hers.

Here, in this tucked-away corner of the room, something sacred is happening: An *inner* bond is forming, the beginning of secure connection.

And then I sense something else from her, so quiet and yet so clear: *I want to leave.*

I feel the truth of it in my body. My work is done here. I have no reason to continue to pretend.

Sometimes the brave thing to do is to stay in a room and do the inner—and outer—work. Other times, the brave thing to do is to excuse yourself, to give yourself permission to leave a room that will always feel like a misfit.[2] I don't owe this space my presence. And I don't have to prove anything by staying.

I rise slowly. I gather my things. The bag I once held like a shield now rests lightly on my shoulder. The heels that felt too tall now feel dignified and poised.

As I walk with her out of the hall, out of the auditorium, and out of the conference, I sense God's presence.

God is with us. We are a little trio of Love: the young teen, the grown woman, and the Presence who never left us.

She pauses inside me, puzzled. *But if God is with us . . . how can God also be in that auditorium?*

I look over at the hands I can still see waving in the distance.

Because Love is bigger than you and me. God can be with those who encounter Love in crowds and concerts and want to stay, and God can be with us who prefer the quiet as we walk away. God's presence isn't scarce.

She is delighted by this answer. By the bigness of a God who can both stay with the other women and leave with us, simultaneously.

GOD CAN BE WITH THOSE WHO ENCOUNTER LOVE IN CROWDS AND CONCERTS AND WANT TO STAY, AND GOD CAN BE WITH US WHO PREFER THE QUIET AS WE WALK AWAY. GOD'S PRESENCE ISN'T SCARCE.

That's all it was.

Just a quiet moment in the back row of a crowded auditorium.

No grand epiphany. No dramatic breakthrough.

And yet, something real shifted that day. I *recognized* her ache.

Up there in the balcony, I realized this part of me wasn't being difficult. She was making a bid for connection.

INNER BIDS FOR CONNECTION

One of my favorite insights from relationship experts John and Julie Gottman is the idea of *bids* for connection.[3] These bids are the small, everyday invitations we offer to the people we love:

"Look at that beautiful robin out in the yard!"

"It's been a long day."

"Do you want to sit with me for a minute?"

"Hello."

These bids may seem insignificant, but they are *everything* when it comes to forging a close, attached relationship.

When someone responds with presence—"*I see it too,*" or, "*Tell me more*"—a thread of connection is strengthened.

But when those bids are missed, or ignored, disconnection grows.

What I want you to understand, dear reader, is that this principle is true not just in marriages or in relationships, but *inside you too.*

Because here's the thing: You don't only offer bids outwardly, to other people. They're also coming from inside you.

Parts of your own inner world are constantly reaching toward you, offering tiny, unspoken *bids* for connection.

A flash of anxiety.

A pang of loneliness.

A sudden pull to withdraw, or fold in on yourself.

These aren't just moods or random emotions. *They are places within, asking to be seen.* They're parts of your own soul bidding for connection, just like a partner might when they reach for your hand or point out a bird on the windowsill.

Just this morning, for example, I found myself checking my phone incessantly. I couldn't figure out why. Suddenly, I realized:

I'm disconnected.

I need to know I'm not alone.

Some part of me is searching for the grounding of connection.

And while a phone is *never* going to fill that void, the desire for connection beneath that action was real.

How many times throughout your day do you reach for something, or someone, in an effort to feel connected? Your phone, a snack, a task. A friend or partner. The impulse itself isn't the problem; it's a clue. *Your soul needs something in that moment*, even though you're not always consciously aware of what it is.

Which brings us back to the simple brilliance of the Gottmans' work.

A relationship grows strong when two people learn to recognize even the smallest signals and say, "I'm here," or, "Yes, I see it too."

Your inner world works in the exact same way.

Every hidden ache, every surge of worry, every tug toward distraction is a part of you whispering:

"Do you see me?"

"Will you meet me here?"

When you notice these bids with kindness, with even a *moment* of awareness, something inside you softens. The distance narrows. A thread is rewoven.

You begin to *meet yourself* with the same care and presence you might offer someone you love. And in that tender moment, something sacred stirs. A space opens up for Love to enter in.

The truth is, your inner world is always reaching out for connection. The question becomes, How do you begin to recognize your soul's bids?

YOUR INNER SOUL MOUNTAIN

Imagine your soul as a mountain.

Not a desolate place, but a wild and beautiful realm, full of distinct terrain. There are sunlit meadows and shadowed caves, rocky cliffs and quiet coves. It's not flat or simple. It's layered. Alive. In motion.

These contours of your soul reflect your entire life, the different seasons, eras, and places where you felt alone, or where love came in. Places where you learned to protect, or to hide. And places where you also learned to hope.

And within each of these terrains lives a different part of you, each one shaped by the landscape it inhabits.

Some parts of you are hunkered down, lost, in the thick forest, unsure how to find their way out.

Some are tucked into shadowy caves, places within where they've learned to hide out of fear or shame.

Some live close to the rocky cliffs, alert, vigilant, always standing guard.

These parts of your soul are not mistakes. They're not problems to solve. They're places within where you're still struggling, yes, but not because your soul is broken.

These parts of you are struggling because they're still stuck in old ways, old places from the past. Places where they've been neglected, hurt, or misunderstood. By others, and also, at times, by you. They haven't yet learned that they can find a new path, a way out of these lonely places into the warmth of connectedness.

What if, instead of calling these parts of your soul selfish or wayward or lost, you named them for what they are—*treasures in exile*?

Because here's the thing: Each lonely, weary, or aching part of your soul, each treasure waiting to be found, is reaching out, longing to be met.

They may not speak in words, but they do send signals,

tiny cues that something hurts, something's off, or something *matters.* A sudden irritation. A wave of dread. An urge to withdraw. A craving for approval. These are not random disruptions. They're *inner bids for connection.*

When you turn toward these bids with compassion, a path of safety, of love, of security is built, or strengthened, within your soul.

When you turn away by ignoring, dismissing, or shaming these parts of yourself, those inner ruptures deepen.

The beautiful truth of your inner soul mountain is this: Just as you can get to know a familiar terrain, a favorite place, or an old path you love to wander, you can also begin to recognize the patterns of your soul. You can learn the distinct movements, familiar voices, and sometimes not-so-helpful ways you protect, long for, and reach for connection.

Here's some insight into my own soul mountain. These are the parts of my inner terrain I've learned to notice when I feel disconnected.

In the middle of the forest sits the Controller—intense, efficient, quick to action, and slow to rest. She clears trails, scans for danger, and tries to keep the whole mountain running on sheer willpower. When she's anxious, she gets sharp. But underneath? She's scared. Scared that if she lets go, everything will fall apart. What looks like strength is really a heavy weight she's learned to carry: *I'm the only one you can trust.*

Down in a dark, cool cave lives the Shadow. When connection feels out of reach, she pulls the fog around her. In my case, that means scrolling, snacking, or one more episode . . .

anything to dull the sting. But beneath the numbing is something deeper: anger, shame, the raw pain of feeling unseen. She disappears not because she wants to be alone, but because she's afraid she's the problem. Her withdrawal is a form of protection: *I'm safest when I'm alone.*

And then there's the Young One—playful, tender, unguarded. She dances barefoot on the sunlit ridge where wildflowers bloom and wonder still feels possible. She only emerges when it feels safe, when connection is close and the air is filled with Love.

This is the inner landscape of my soul. And my guess is that yours isn't so different.

Each place within holds a story.

Each part of you is bidding—sometimes awkwardly, sometimes urgently—for connection.

Your longings may come wrapped in urgency, irritation, exhaustion, or restlessness.

But here's what I need you to know: None of these parts are broken. They are treasures in exile, pieces of your soul longing to be reclaimed and reconnected.

And your work is to listen for their bids.

To learn the language of your inner world.

To recognize: *A part of me is hurting.*

To return to connection: *I'm here. I see you. You belong with me.*

This is the beginning of *inner* repair.

Maybe not yet with the person who hurt you.

Maybe not even with God, at least not yet.

But with someone you may have overlooked entirely: *yourself.*

BECOMING A SECURE SOUL

This way of understanding ourselves—as made up of different parts, each carrying their own story and longing for connection—has been the most helpful tool I've found for making sense of disconnection.[4]

It rests on a simple truth echoed across psychology, philosophy, and Scripture: We are multifaceted beings.[5] Our souls aren't monoliths. They're more like living ecosystems, interconnected places within us, each with its own fears, beliefs, burdens, and ways of surviving.

And these parts of your soul don't only need other people. They need *you*. You are not a bystander in your inner life. You are a participant.

At the center of your soul mountain is your core self—your God-created self, the image of God in you (Gen. 1:27). It's that quiet inner place within where you catch glimpses of calm, where perspective returns, where you can hold what's true without running from it.[6] Not a perfected version of you, just the truest, most grounded place in you.[7]

For some of us, the language of "self" can feel complicated. We've heard enough self-centered messaging in the modern world to be wary. But the alternative isn't to erase the self. Scripture paints a more honest tension: We are wonderfully made (Ps. 139:14) and image-bearing, and we are also wounded and in need of healing. Paul himself doesn't describe the self as something to be erased, but as something to be transformed—"crucified with Christ" (Gal. 2:20) and also "raised with Christ" (Col. 3:1). His language points to restoration, not annihilation. And Jesus, when asked about the greatest commandment, wove selfhood into the very fabric of spiritual formation: "Love your neighbor as yourself" (Mark 12:31). To neglect the self is to neglect the very soil from which love of neighbor is meant to grow.

Neuroscience also highlights the remarkable nature of the human self: The human brain contains highly developed regions in the prefrontal cortex that support *conscious self-awareness*, including the capacity to step back, observe what's happening inside, reflect on it, and *choose how to respond*.[8] You might think of this capacity as wisdom, attentiveness, self-awareness, or agency. Regardless, this observing "self" is not a distortion of faith but a miracle of creation, a biological echo of the spiritual center Christians have long described as the soul.

JUST AS YOU CAN GET TO KNOW A FAMILIAR TERRAIN, A FAVORITE PLACE, OR AN OLD PATH YOU LOVE TO WANDER, YOU CAN ALSO BEGIN TO RECOGNIZE THE PATTERNS OF YOUR SOUL.

And here's the wonder of your design: This observing "self" is capable of *recognizing* the parts of you that have been lost, exiled, or disconnected. You can learn to turn toward them with the same kind of presence and warmth you would offer someone you love.

Just as you join with God in extending care to others, you can also join with God in extending care to the parts of your own soul.

In this way, *you* become a kind of internal attachment figure for your own soul. You become the one who sees, welcomes, and tends to what has been pushed aside. You become the agent of recognition, the one who learns to notice disconnection and tell the truth:

I'm not okay.

I'm lonely.

I'm upset.

You can become a compassionate witness *to your own experience*—the one who recognizes disconnection and makes the choice to return, always, to Love. You won't do it perfectly, but perfection was never the point.

Often, the deepest repair begins right there, when *you* recognize the ache:

I see you.

I'm here now.

You don't have to be alone anymore.

This is the sacred, ongoing work of *inner* attachment, what I call *becoming a secure soul.*

Recognize: *I'm lonely.*

Recognize: *I'm angry.*

Recognize: *I'm scared.*

And while *you* are essential to this process, don't think for a moment that you're doing this work alone.

You are not a single parent to your soul. None of us is.

THE LOVING PRESENCE AT THE CENTER

The truth is, you don't set out on this journey of reclaiming lost parts of your soul alone. That's not how you were made.

You were never meant to take this journey by yourself.

Someone goes with you, clearing the path ahead, giving you courage, and, at times, even carrying you.

This someone is God—Love incarnate, the One who is Spirit and yet took on flesh, who once walked among us in Jesus and still moves within us through the power of the Spirit. The One who, as Scripture says, *is* Love (1 John 4:8, 16).

A God who is not only "out there" in the heavens but also alive within the inner recesses of your soul, like a radiant flame in a mountain sanctuary. From there, light spills into every forest path, every shadowed cave, every fractured place.

Imagine this:

A loving Presence steps into your inner soul mountain to reclaim every single lost part of you. Jesus moves along rugged pathways, searches through every cave, calls out across the rocky cliffs, and combs through dense forests.

He is not rushed and is not afraid of what he finds. He is steady, intentional, and unshaken. He will go into the deepest, most broken places to bring healing warmth to what has been lost, left alone, or disconnected.

And when he finds these unclaimed parts of you, he is patient, gentle, and kind. Because at first, they are like frightened creatures in the wild. *They don't know what Love is like.*

They don't know if they can trust him.

But he stays. Not forcing, not judging, just offering the steady warmth of secure presence.

And as each part of your soul slowly starts to trust him, he gathers them and brings them home.

Home, as it turns out, is not a fortress but a feast. At the center of the mountain, the sanctuary opens into a sunlit meadow. A long table is spread with fruit, warm bread, and sparkling drinks. It's a feast of welcome. A feast of togetherness, of belonging.

Here, each now-claimed treasure takes her seat of honor, welcomed by the Source of Love, the One who brings all things back into connection.

The Controller begins to sense what it feels like to be held by someone stronger than herself. She exhales, releases her grip, and turns her face toward the sun.

The Shadow, no longer hidden in the dark with shame, begins to shimmer with a shy sort of joy. She's learning what it feels like to receive Love's compassion.

And the Young One, wide-eyed with wonder, steps into the light at the center of it all, dancing with delight before the One who loves her.

There's no shame at this banquet. No judgment.

Only delight in these quirky, sometimes ragged, always beautiful parts of your own soul finally gathered in the Presence of Love, finally sensing what it means to belong to God and to one another.

Each part of you is distinct. And each part of you is thrilled to be gathered with the others.

It's a glimpse of the greater feast that awaits when every part of you, and every soul gathered at last into Love, is welcomed into the heavenly mountain sanctuary.

A quiet warmth, dazzling and steady, spreads through you.

You feel vulnerable, yet safe.

"I don't want you to leave," you whisper.

And he doesn't.

Instead, he stays, right there at the center.

Grace keeps flowing, as your whole soul, every hidden place, bathes in the goodness of being fully welcomed, fully seen, fully loved.

And slowly, gently, you begin to change.

Not by force.

Not by effort.

But by Love.

You are becoming someone new.

No longer fragmented or lost.

No longer filled with blame or shame.

But whole.

A person filled with Love—the most powerful kind of person there is.

Recognize: *A part of me is disconnected.*

Return: *I am loved, even here.*

PART TWO

HOW YOUR SOUL ADAPTS

CHAPTER 4

MEET THE CONTROLLER WITHIN

I can still see her, sitting alone in a dimly lit classroom, hunched over a desk where the plastic seat is bolted to the worn plywood surface. It's the kind of desk you find in middle schools everywhere, scarred with years of doodles and gum wads, fluorescent lights flickering overhead.

She's fourteen, maybe fifteen. Ponytail tight. Braces in place. Flannel shirt rolled up at the sleeves. Her pencil moves furiously across a page of algebra problems like her life depends on it.

Because, in a way, it does.

She's not trying to impress anyone. She's not looking for attention or praise. She's just trying to survive.

This is the Controller part of my soul who learned that safety meant staying self-sufficient. *Don't get too close. Don't let anyone see too much. If I can stay in control, I won't get hurt.*

She avoids vulnerability, not so much out of pride, but out of protection. She solves problems before they start. She keeps everything running smoothly. She doesn't ask for help because needing others feels dangerous.

She works hard, relentlessly at times, because the idea of needing someone, of being exposed or dependent, feels too risky.

In my case, the Controller tends toward avoidance. She helps me prevent pain through downplaying emotional needs and suppressing vulnerability. But make no mistake, underneath all her efforts to stay safe is a deeper fear that she's not worthy of connection.

THE WALLS WE BUILD

It's evening. My husband and I are supposed to be winding down for the night, relaxing in the living room before bed. But I'm hunched over my laptop, shoulders so tight you could bounce a penny off them. My body is clenched, my focus razor-sharp.

I'm frantically *not* relaxing.

He walks over and places his hands on my shoulders. Years ago, I would have tensed up even more, or muttered, "*I have to get this done,*" in that clipped, distracted tone he knows too well. But he's brave. He risks it anyway.

And I've learned a little.

This time, I let my shoulders soften. My eyes well with tears.

"I'm tired," I whisper.

"Can't you stop?" he asks.

The Controller inside of me doesn't think I can.

But I'm learning to pause. To notice. To wonder: *Can I?*

The next morning, I am journaling and I ask God to help me understand this part of myself. I want to know where this relentless intensity comes from.

And suddenly, I'm back there. With that young fourteen-year-old version of myself. The one in that dimly lit classroom, hunched over the desk that's bolted to a worn plywood surface. Ponytail tight. Pencil moving furiously across the page of algebra problems.

She hasn't noticed me yet. She's only vaguely aware of her classmates, since she's mostly shut them out. Her focus is absolute.

I linger as I take her in like a loving parent, absorbed by her presence. I'm amazed by her. By her tenacity. Her laser focus. Her drive to solve hard problems.

I'm also concerned for her.

She's so young, just a child. Is she aware of how tense her body is? Of how she's shutting out the world around her?

Her presence is familiar to me—*very* familiar. She nearly drove me into the ground halfway through my doctoral program. And I didn't stop her then because I didn't know how.

But I know her better now.

I kneel beside her at her desk, not intrusively, just quietly. Gently.

Honey, I say, *you don't have to work so hard.*

She looks up. Her eyes soften.

She's beginning to trust me. Not everyone. Not yet. But me? Maybe.

What are you afraid might happen if you stop? I ask, my voice low and curious.

She shrugs, a little wistful.

I don't know, is what I sense from her. *This is just what I do. It's the only way I know.*

I want to scoop her into my arms. But I know she wouldn't like that. She's skittish. Cautious. Like a young colt that's ready to bolt at the slightest motion.

So I stay with her. Still. Curious.

Are you aware of your peers over there? I'm trying to gain deeper understanding.

She glances toward the shadowy outlines at the edge of her view. She's aware. But it's as if she cannot get herself to join them.

I sense a loneliness from her.

I don't need other people, she says, gesturing to her books. *I need to solve these problems.*

My mind flashes to my life now. I think about how often I forego a social gathering, or even just a phone call with a friend, for my laptop. How often I choose my work over interaction.

I get it. There's comfort in staying focused on math problems. For one thing, they're solvable.

People are not.

They're messy.

They reach for things I'm not sure I can give.

I used to beat up on this part of myself for staying so siloed off. So hidden away from other people. *Why can't you just be normal?!*

But sitting with her now, I see her more fully. It takes a lot for her to leave the safety of her desk and step into that crowd of noisy, buzzing teenagers.

And it dawns on me: It's not so much that she's trying to keep control.

It's that she's trying to keep me safe.

She learned early that people are unpredictable, especially their emotions. The shifting moods, unspoken tensions, the undercurrents—it all overwhelms her. She doesn't know what to do with it.

So she turns to the security of structure: lists, homework, math problems.

They're not just tasks. They're walls of safety that are contained and predictable.

Not because she doesn't long for connection.

But because she has found this to be the safer path: focused, on the edges, where the risks are lower and the rules are clear.

As I notice this gently, without judgment, she begins to relax.

She feels seen.

It's overwhelming, I sense from her. *It's just easier to stay by myself.*

And I get it.

Even now, this part of me still resists social gatherings, despite other parts of me that genuinely want to enjoy them. As an adult, I've found that walking into a party as a therapist can feel like being a surgeon in a room full of gaping wounds. You're expected to ignore the wounds and make *small talk*. At a Super Bowl party, I don't just see the food and the games. I see the heartbreaks. The masks. The hidden pain.

So initially, I'm cautious. Careful. Always a few steps back, quietly monitoring the emotional weather in the room. Over time, I find my comfort zones, places where I freely enter in. But it's still a lot of work.

I turn back toward her, this younger version of myself, with a better sense of what middle school was like for her.

I understand, I say. *It's not that you don't like people. It's that it's hard to relax around them. It's stressful. You take a lot in.*

She's still sitting at her desk, but we're connected now. She's no longer focused on her math problems. She's with me.

I am seeing her in a new light. And I'm feeling incredibly compassionate for her.

Because underneath her desire for control is *fear*—the kind of unsettled feeling every single human has on some level, even if you are not a therapist at heart or particularly sensitive. The ache that whispers:

They might not understand me.

They might not see me.

They might ask more of me than I can give.

So this part of me learned to keep to herself. *If I don't let anyone in*, she reasons, *I can't be hurt. Overwhelmed. Rejected.*

But she's also tired. And so very often, she feels alone.

THE ATTACHMENT ROOTS OF CONTROL

The Controller part of you might not sit at a desk doing algebra problems in a dimly lit room, but there is a younger version of you who stands guard within your soul. We all carry some version of this Inner Controller—the part of you who learned to prevent pain by staying one step ahead, managing what you can, downplaying what you feel, or trying to get things exactly right. Her presence doesn't mean something is wrong with you. It means your system learned how to stay safe when love or connection felt risky.

Your brain is wired to seek predictability, especially in relationships.[1] When love feels inconsistent, your nervous system learns to stay on alert, to scan, brace, and manage. And your inner world carries those memories, both from today, and also from the past, where you learned it wasn't safe to need too much, feel too much, or ask for care.[2]

WHAT LOOKS LIKE OVERFUNCTIONING IN ADULTHOOD OFTEN TRACES BACK TO A YOUNGER SELF WHO LEARNED EARLY, AND FOR GOOD REASON, THAT STAYING IN CHARGE FELT SAFER THAN STAYING OPEN.

Maybe you became the responsible one, the peacekeeper, the one who could sense what was needed before anyone said a word. However it happened, your system registered: *I'm on my own here.* And a part of you stepped in—not out of malice, but out of mercy.

This young Inner Controller became the parent to your inner world (and in some cases to everyone else around her) before your brain was fully formed, before you had the capacity to process the weight you were carrying. She learned to monitor, anticipate, and push through. In short, she learned to overfunction. Competence turned into compulsion.

Control became her way of *managing* connection from a distance, without having to risk need, vulnerability, or uncertainty.

What looks like overfunctioning in adulthood often traces back to a younger self who learned early, and for good reason, that staying in charge felt safer than staying open. These early attempts to gain control aren't weakness. They're intelligence.

The goal isn't to get rid of her intelligence or drive. The goal is to notice *when that strength becomes self-protection at the cost of connection.*

At her core, your Inner Controller has always been guarding against one thing: the pain of disconnection. She doesn't yet know that *you are here for her now. You* are that adult presence who can listen, respond, and stay. And in many cases, she doesn't yet trust that *God is here too*, and that care can remain even when needs are expressed or messy feelings spill over. So she continues to manage closeness the only way she knows how. She tries to control the terms:

If I meet everyone's needs before they ask, I won't get hurt—or left.

If I never show what I really feel, no one can use it against me.

If I stay two steps ahead, I won't get caught off guard.

And here is the truth: *She's still with you.* Traces of her are still etched in your soul. Your work now is not to silence her or overpower her, but to recognize her bids for connection, and to gently teach her that there is someone who can hold what was never hers to carry.

THE CONTROLLER'S BIDS FOR CONNECTION

The Controller rarely says, *I'm scared*, or *I need help*. Instead, she speaks through overworking. Through saying yes when your soul longs to say no. Through nodding along with opinions most of you doesn't actually agree with, just to keep a peace she doesn't know how to break.

Her bids for connection aren't always graceful.

In my own life, they show up as a ferocious pull to overfunction. When I'm alone, that means overworking. When I'm with other people, it means over-caretaking, an almost compulsive urgency to anticipate needs before anyone has to ask. I can feel her kick in when I walk into a room full of people, when a conversation veers into unpredictability, or when I notice the slightest shift in someone's tone and feel compelled to make it better.

On the outside, I seem together. But underneath, my shoulders are tight. My jaw is clenched. I am vigilant, tense, on watch. I don't even notice it until someone reaches toward me, like my husband rubbing my shoulders, and I flinch. I abruptly change the topic. Or worse, I lash out at *him,* the very person daring to interrupt my compulsive overfunctioning.

For a long time, I thought this was just how I was wired.

I thought it was normal to overfunction with other people, then retreat in exhaustion. But over time, I've learned to see that urgency for what it is—a signal from my Inner Controller. It's a cue that she needs *me* to show up as the adult in the room, and to gently help her hand over the reins. Not to shame her, but to *parent* her.

I see how hard you're working.

It's okay.

It's not actually your job to hold everyone together.

Maybe you've noticed these bids too. Your Controller works overtime to keep things from unraveling, because she never learned there was someone who could help her. And here's the good news: *You* are that someone. You can learn to recognize her bids and respond with care.

Sometimes, her strategy is to move toward connection through effort. You might find yourself micromanaging conversations, scanning for the tiniest signs of disapproval, or bending over backward because you don't want to feel left out. She might keep you up late replaying what you said in a conversation; or she might analyze, problem solve, or perfect, hoping that if she can just get it right, you'll finally feel secure.

Other times, her strategy is to move away from connection. She tries to protect you through creating distance. You might find yourself pulling back, keeping your guard up, or carefully curating what you share. She encourages you to swallow your hurt, hide your tears, or say "I'm fine," because showing too much feels like it could cost too much.[3]

And sometimes you do both: You reach out one minute and retreat the next. You do anything to manage the unpredictability of love.

Whether your Inner Controller clings or retreats, she's not trying to sabotage you. She's trying to keep you safe. She works to create the illusion of stability in a world that often feels uncertain or chaotic.

The problem is: While her tactics might create a temporary sense of order, they also shut down the very things that make real connection possible: flexibility, openness, and trust.

Imagine a lifeguard scanning the water—hyperalert, never off duty, always watching for signs of danger. She's perched high in her chair, eyes darting from swimmer to swimmer, adrenaline always humming.

She doesn't rest. She doesn't blink. She doesn't trust anyone else to see what she sees.

At first, it looks noble, protective, selfless, and strong. But hours pass. Days. She won't come down, not even for water. Her skin is sunburned. Her muscles ache. And still, she refuses to raise her hand and ask for relief.

She's terrified that the moment she steps down, everything will fall apart.

What she doesn't realize is that her vigilance, the very thing she thought would keep you safe, is starting to cause harm.

Please hear me say: Your Inner Controller is not the enemy. She's smart. Hardworking. Adaptive. Fiercely loyal. She stepped in when you needed her most. *She was always trying to help.*

And yet, heartbreakingly, the very strategies that once kept you safe can start to keep you small—protected from harm, but also cut off from rest, softness, and play. Cut off from the very connection you were made to enjoy.

So the signals grow louder, especially the overfunctioning, the exhaustion, the perfecting, the pleasing. That persistent sense that something is missing, even when you're doing everything "right."

Remember, those signals aren't the enemy.

They're invitations. Inner bids for *connection*.

What she needs most isn't tighter control. It's secure presence. And *you* are the first point of contact.

Connection begins when you recognize her ache and help her name what she can't:

You're exhausted.

You're overwhelmed.

You're working so hard.

Not to criticize her, but to *see* her. To offer her a lifeline of compassion: *You're not alone anymore. I'm with you.*

And as you meet her with compassion, something beautiful happens. She begins to learn she doesn't have to hold the whole world together to keep you safe. And you begin to understand what she's afraid will happen if she lets go.

She begins to trust you.

A secure *inner* bond begins to form.

WHEN YOUR CONTROLLER MEETS LOVE

It's one thing to identify as a "highly sensitive person," or to name an "anxious attachment style" or a pattern of people-pleasing or perfectionism. These labels can be really helpful in offering language, insight, or a place to begin.

But they're not the same as *being with* the part of you who actually lives it. The one who never got the care she needed.

Head knowledge might open the door, but it doesn't walk you through it. Real transformation begins when you turn toward what's hurting—not to analyze or fix, but to *connect.*

This process starts with you, as you learn to connect with this place within your soul. It's similar to what you'd do if your neighbor were hurting. You'd reach out. Maybe show up at her door with a casserole. You'd listen and offer compassion. In that moment, you become an attachment tether, an agent of God's loving presence.

THE VERY STRATEGIES THAT ONCE KEPT YOU SAFE CAN START TO KEEP YOU SMALL—PROTECTED FROM HARM, BUT ALSO CUT OFF FROM REST, SOFTNESS, AND PLAY.

In the same way, you can extend loving presence toward the hurting parts within you, opening the door to more connection.

So I turn toward this young Inner Controller again, still hunkered down at the place where it all formed.

I'm back in that middle school classroom. The desk is small. The room is dim, institutional. I can smell the pencil shavings (yes, pencil shavings!) and the musty mix of cafeteria food and adolescent angst.

There she is—fourteen, hunched over that algebra worksheet, ponytail pulled tight, the clock ticking too loudly on the wall. Around her, kids whisper and pass notes. She doesn't even flinch. She's solving for *x* like her life depends on it.

Back in that confusing, often unpredictable social jungle—those formative adolescent years when you had to learn to survive mean boys, raging hormones, cryptic girls, social labels, and your own tangled insecurities. No wonder she's so riveted on those algebra problems! Focused like a laser. A little intense, yes. But fierce in her survival mode.

REAL TRANSFORMATION BEGINS WHEN YOU TURN TOWARD WHAT'S HURTING—NOT TO ANALYZE OR FIX, BUT TO *CONNECT.*

I mentally run through my parenting Rolodex: How do you encourage a young teenager you're worried about, but who doesn't really want to let you in?

I know it's not quite right, but I try to offer a direct suggestion: *Don't you want to stop working and join your peers?*

Without missing a beat, she looks up, and I sense her ginormous inner eye roll within me. And then a feeling of her calling out my own hypocrisy: *Really, because you're so good at socializing?*

I burst out laughing. She's got me there. *I know. It's not that simple.*

She likes that I laughed at her eye roll. That I didn't take offense. That I stayed, even though she rolled her eyes at me. That's new to her. She's careful with adults. But she senses something different in me. She senses a strength. And a shared love of sarcasm. Maybe she can trust me.

And just like that, our connection deepens. Not because I asked the perfect question. Not because I fixed anything. But because I *hold steady*. And she feels that.

Sensing her trust, I try again. I tell her what I didn't know I needed to hear back then. What I need to hear even now:

It's okay that you need space sometimes. That you keep to yourself. I know you want to fit in.

I also know you're doing your best to balance it all. I know it's hard. I know sometimes it's lonely. I just want you to know that I see you. And I'm here.

Her eyes well up with tears. They don't fall, but I see them. And she knows that I see them. Our connection feels steady. Unrushed and unforced.

And then a curiosity rises up within me. There's no agenda, no right answer. Just an openness, a wondering.

Where do you feel most safe? I ask her. *Where do you feel like you can breathe?*

She goes quiet. The question lands somewhere beneath the algebra, beneath the ponytail pulled tight, beneath the constant bracing.

And then the classroom fades. The light shifts.

We're outside now, surrounded by tall lodgepole pines that flank our small mountain cabin, the one we've been going to since I was born. The air smells like pine needles and sun-warmed dirt.

I love it here, she says. *This is where I feel God.*

Something in me softens at the tenderness of it. I'd never fully realized that the part of me who finds such peace in nature as an adult has been with me all along. But of course she has.

She's given me a gift—a fuller sense of who I am and who I've always been.

And in that moment, I begin to understand her better. I begin to see what she has always needed.

Beneath the tight grip of control, what she always wanted is simple: *to be known.*

And then, unexpectedly, she gives me one more insight. She pulls out a chessboard, right there in the middle of the woods.

Want to play? she asks.

My heart melts. I nearly laugh aloud.

Even now, as an adult, my husband and I love to play chess, sometimes together, sometimes on our own. I never would've thought to put that on my Match.com profile when I finally started dating again in my thirties. But when he pulls out the board, something lights up in me. It's how we connect without words, how we rest without shutting down, how we take the edge off our shared penchant for analysis and problem-solving.

And suddenly I see it: She also craved a kind of mental play. She longed for a place where focus could be joyful and even shared. She just didn't know how to name it back then. So she felt odd. Different. Incomplete.

The truth is: She was always going to be a problem solver. That was her strategy to keep me safe, even as it was also part of her authentic self.

WHAT'S AUTHENTIC AND STRONG IN ALL OF US CAN ALSO BECOME OUR KRYPTONITE.

Problem solving wasn't the problem. The loneliness was.

Because what's authentic and strong in all of us can also become our kryptonite.

But here, in the steadiness of being seen, I glimpse a

different side of her. There's a playful glint in her eye. A reminder that she isn't only lonely; she also carries joy.

I could not love this magnificent fourteen-year-old girl more.

Back in my adult life, I have tears in my eyes.

My shoulders are relaxed.

My jaw isn't clenched.

I'm at my desk, still working. But something has shifted.

I'm not alone.

I'm connected.

To myself.

To her.

And to God, whose presence has been here all along, even when parts of me couldn't see it.

WHAT A SECURE SOUL NEEDS

When you attune to your Inner Controller, you begin to discover what truly brings you relief, care, or a sense of being held. Not what you think you "should" need or what others say will help. But what genuinely allows the hardest-working part of you to rest, to play, to loosen her grip. These parts of you hold surprising wisdom, when you pause long enough to listen.

In my case, my Controller longed for a walk through the woods, space to breathe, and a cozy mountain place where she could let her guard down, play, and be herself. Yours might crave a room full of people, music, solitude, or movement. The point isn't to prescribe a particular activity, but to facilitate the kind of connection that leads to genuine discovery.

And learning to offer that kind of connection to a part of yourself turns out to be very much like parenting real-life kids. It's the slow work of becoming a steady, trustworthy presence, one who seeks to understand, who welcomes honesty, and who makes room for authentic expression.

From an attachment lens, that kind of inner security grows through three essential qualities: curiosity, compassion, and containment.

Curiosity means you turn toward this part of you with openness instead of judgment. It invites understanding: *I see you. What's happening here? What are you afraid might happen if you stop?* Each moment of gentle curiosity rewires your nervous system toward safety and trust.

Compassion softens the edges. It says, *I know how hard you're working. It makes sense. You've been carrying a lot.* Compassion quiets the body's inner alarm system and mirrors the warmth of God's presence within you.

CULTIVATING A SECURE SOUL ISN'T ABOUT *ELIMINATING CONTROL.* IT'S ABOUT GUIDING THIS PART OF YOUR SOUL TOWARD CONNECTION.

Containment brings steadiness and structure and the assurance that you are the adult in your soul. It's not control or criticism, but calm strength: *I can hold this. It's okay to slow down. You don't have to carry this alone.* Like a loving parent, you create safety and space for rest and renewal.

When curiosity, compassion, and containment come

together, your Inner Controller begins to trust that she no longer has to work quite so hard.

She'll still be vigilant, and she'll still persist on your behalf. But now, she's learning what it means to operate *within a loving ecosystem*, one in which she is anchored, supported, and held.

Because now she has *you.*

And a God who stays.

As she establishes a secure *inner* attachment with you and God, she begins to trust. And over time, she learns how to let other people in as well.

Cultivating a secure soul isn't about *eliminating control.* It's about guiding this part of your soul toward connection.

It's about meeting her at heart level, listening for her cues, and gently showing her:

You don't have to hold this all alone anymore.

Recognize: *I'm grasping for control.*

Return: *I am loved, even here.*

CHAPTER 5

LOVE YOUR INNER SHADOW

As your Controller begins to loosen her grip, even just a little, you may notice another part rising to take her place. She has an entirely different agenda, and her presence creates a new kind of inner tension.

She doesn't come with spreadsheets or schedules. She's not trying to keep you in line.

She's trying to *break out of the lines*—to shatter the cage you've built for yourself on the inside.

I call her the Shadow.

Where the Controller works overtime to keep you safe, the Shadow shows up to help you cope with painful feelings, though not always in healthy ways. She craves release, relief, and comfort. She's the part of you who whispers,

Why do I always have to be the responsible one?

You deserve it!

I need to feel something.

Let me have this one thing.

She's not trying to harm you, and she's not out to hurt anyone else. She's trying to bring *relief*, to restore something that's been lost in the only way she knows how. The Shadow surfaces when tender emotions like longing, loneliness, and shame have been buried for too long and start to rise up in your soul. In that moment, the Shadow moves fast, doing whatever it takes to ease the ache.

The Shadow is often the place inside we'd rather hide. She carries the feelings we think we're not supposed to have, feelings like anger, envy, desire, shame. While the Controller manages things on the surface, the Shadow simmers underneath. And when she finally breaks through, her actions tend to come out sideways through escape, self-sabotage, impulsiveness, chaotic thoughts, or shutting down completely.

This part of you often takes root in early relationships where love and fear get tangled together. She wants connection but does not know how to trust it. She longs to be seen but also braces for rejection. She can feel shameful, like a secret you keep tucked away. And yet, she's trying to say something true:

I've been hurt, and I don't know where to take that pain.

That bid for connection—wrapped in fear, longing, and heartache—often shows up in unwanted ways. Sometimes, these shadowy feelings surface in therapy or in prayer, but more often, they make themselves known when you find yourself doing something you wish you wouldn't.

UNDERNEATH THE FANTASY

Much to my embarrassment, I've just binge-watched an entire season of *Love Island USA*. I'm watching Gen Z islanders prance around in bikinis, lip fillers, and hair extensions with a strange mix of horror and delight, rooting for real human souls to shine through, even as I gasp when they don't.

The Controller in me explains it away by saying I'm "doing research" as a psychologist. *Ha!* But if I'm honest, the truth is that another part of me secretly admires how unrestrained they are.

Unfiltered. Unapologetic. With their bodies. With their f-bombs. With their feelings.

Don't get me wrong. I know there are wounds and insecurities hidden beneath unfiltered bravado.

But still, the truth is that a part of me is captivated. Envious, even. It stirs something old and familiar. A fantasy part of my brain kicks in, an escape hatch I've relied on since I was very young.

Because underneath the Controller—long before I fell in love with the order and logic of algebra—there was another love. A secret one.

Romance novels. Soap operas. *Days of Our Lives*. (Bo and Hope, anyone?) *Sweet Valley High*—every single one. And all the syrupy, slow-burn teenage romance sagas: anything filled with longing glances, first dates, and the hope that love might save the day.

I adored them all. Every last one.

And since soap operas and *Sweet Valley High* books weren't allowed in my household, I hid them. I'd record *Days of Our Lives* on a VHS tape and wait for those rare, precious moments when my mom was visiting a neighbor or out at the grocery store to sneak in an episode.

Or, during our annual back-to-school shopping trip to the mall in Billings, Montana, I'd bide my time until no one was watching in the bookstore. I knew exactly where to find the young adult shelves, mid-level back wall, where the *Sweet Valley High* books were lined up in perfect order. I'd quietly grab the next number off the shelf, slip my hard-earned dollar bills across the counter, and tuck the book into my yellow purse. Then I'd smuggle my treasure home and hide it in my secret spot: a shoebox buried deep in a cubbyhole inside my sister's bedroom closet. No one had a clue.

Tucked far beneath the radar of my strict Inner Controller, there was another part of me that longed for love. She lived in the fantasy that someone, somewhere, would see me . . . and choose me.

The only problem was, while those stories lit up my imagination, I had no idea how to live them out in real life.

Boys didn't flirt with me in hallways.

No one passed me notes or made grand gestures at my locker. I was awkward. Shy. Unsure of what to say or how to be with boys.

So when I find myself in my fifties, binge-watching teenage romance melodrama like *Love Island*, and I notice a harsh inner voice telling me how ridiculous I am—I pause.

I recognize: *I'm craving something.*

I return: *I am loved, even here.*

And sometimes, returning to love means facing not only the part of me who dreamed of being chosen, but also the part who didn't know what to do with all the ache when she wasn't.

The part who didn't fall into a love story, but fell into self-loathing. Who didn't find a boy to see her, but found a journal to scream the f-word into.

Because underneath the sweet, secret fantasy life was another part of the Shadow. And this one stayed hidden in the darker corners, where longing morphed into shame, and unmet desire turned on itself.

THE TWO FACES OF THE SHADOW

The Shadow part of you often begins as a minor, manageable ache. You might notice a longing for pleasure, comfort, or recognition. These feelings are completely human. In fact, they're often attachment longings that show up as a craving for connection, a desire to be seen, or a moment of relief from the weight of responsibility.

***EVERY PART OF YOU* IS WIRED FOR CONNECTION— EVEN YOUR SHADOWY EMOTIONS.**

But when that part of you is met with shame, silence, or rejection—when she is not met with loving presence in those initial manifestations—she intensifies. Often she goes underground. And that's when her attempts to self-soothe begin to show up in more destructive ways.

What starts as a genuine longing becomes compulsion.

What starts as a need for comfort becomes self-sabotage.

What starts as a flicker of envy becomes a raging blaze of bitterness or resentment.

This shift happens for so many of us, not because we're broken or weak, but because *every part of you* is wired for connection—even your shadowy emotions. When that initial bid for connection is threatened or shamed, the Shadow doubles down and burrows deeper into the recesses of your soul, far away from Love's containing presence.

And in doing so, she often takes on a more chaotic form. She might lash out at others. She might numb out in increasingly destructive ways. She might shut you down through self-sabotage, rage scrolling, or binge-watching endless hours of TV. Or she might quietly simmer inside your soul with envy, anger, or resentment.

But even then, beneath the chaos, her cry is still the same:

I'm hurting. And I don't know where to take that pain.

And so, as I reflect on my long-standing penchant for the escape hatch of love fantasy, I also reconnect with a more painful, shadowy set of feelings, the ones that came after the fantasy faded.

Because eventually, the gap between what I dreamed of and what I actually experienced became too wide to hold. The escape hatch collapsed. And all that longing, with nowhere safe to go, turned inward.

I can still feel echoes of her pain.

THE F-WORD

Instead of berating myself for binge-watching Netflix, I decide to turn my attention to this place within. The one who craved a fantasy of love that felt so out of reach.

And almost immediately I sense her presence still within me. She's about fourteen years old, but unlike the Controller, she shows up somewhere else entirely—sprawled out on the floor of her new "big girl" bedroom on the second floor of my childhood home. I'd recently moved up into this room that used to be our guest room, graduating from the little girl's room with orange flowers next door to my parents' downstairs.

This new room feels grown-up. The walls are wrapped in yellow wallpaper lined with pale columns and soft blue flowers along the bottom.

In my mind, this teenage part of me is big and forceful. But as I connect with her now, she seems so tiny. So alone.

It's evening, after dinner, and in the warm light behind a closed bedroom door, she has pulled out her cloth-covered journal and is pressing her ballpoint pen so hard into the pages, it tears a rip right through them.

And I remember:

She didn't cut herself.

She cut the paper.

F@&#$?&!!!!

I don't know whether to laugh or cry, seeing her so upset as she scratches this word into the paper. She's so tiny and yet so intense in her emotion.

Also . . .

Where did she even learn to use the f-bomb? This was before the word was trendy or tossed around for effect. She hadn't heard it in movies, that's for sure. She wasn't allowed to see movies like that. And she didn't hear it at home.

But somehow, it was the word she felt. It's still the word I feel at times, though my Inner Controller rarely lets me say the word out loud.

I can see the screaming capital letters, the ink looping and slashing across the page—so dark, so violent, it looks like bruises. Literally cutting through the paper.

I haven't always known how to connect with this part of me. For years, she loomed large in my mind. I tried to keep her locked away, to banish her to a lonely cave within my soul.

It feels awkward to sit with her now. Uncomfortable. A little shameful.

And I realize those feelings are coming from another part of me—my devoted Inner Controller is ready to step in. It's she who wants to banish this part of me far away. After all, she's the "good girl" inside me, and to her, this shadowy part feels like a threat.

So I turn toward that Inner Controller with compassion. I acknowledge her fears that if she lets this part of me in, something bad might happen. I honor her desire to help. And I also offer her loving containment, reminding her of what God has been teaching me: *This shadowy one also needs my presence.*

Something in her softens.

Feeling more settled and open, I turn my attention back to the young shadow part of my soul, where the blaze of anger and pain still simmers. I ask God to help me see her more clearly.

And in that spaciousness, I realize she's not scary at all. She is so very *young.*

As I offer her compassion, I notice she isn't mostly angry. She's *hurting.*

Memories start to flash through my mind.

My locker mate's boyfriend with the mean streak—the one who crafted a tiny bra out of walnut shells and rubber bands and held it up in front of a mocking crowd of boys between classes at our school. "A tiny bra for a tiny girl," he announced, smirking as he held up his creation for all to see before handing it to me.

Or the day I got my period at fifteen, much later than all my friends, and bled through my black checkered pants. Of course, he was the one who noticed that too. "Hey Toothpick, did you sit on a pack of chewed-up Big Red?" he yelled across the schoolyard.

I played it cool, laughing along with the joke. "It's fine!" I said to my friends, trying not to make a scene.

But inside, I was mortified. Humiliated. A quiet, relentless shame settled in. In my young eyes, *I* was to blame. My body most of all. It was the reason boys didn't notice me, or worse, laughed at me. The reason the teenage love my peers seemed to be finding felt so out of reach for me.

Outwardly, I was too ashamed to let anyone know how I really felt. I wouldn't have known how to name the hatred I felt toward my body. No one talked this way back then, not even the well-meaning adults who loved me. But in that journal, this young shadowy part of me let it all out.

God, why did you make me like this? she scrawled in ink, deep into those pages. *I hate myself.*

F@&#$?&!!!!

Sometimes her fantasies took a dark turn. She imagined disappearing or vanishing completely, planning elaborate funerals.

Then they'll finally see me! she wrote again, the ink etching deep.

I didn't want to die. I just wanted to be valued.

I continue to take in this younger version of myself as she rage journals. I take in her tightly permed brown hair, her crooked front teeth covered in metal, her tiny toothpick body. A late bloomer, her parents would say. *It's better not to bloom in middle school.* An observation that is likely true, and that steadied other parts of me. But it didn't help *her.*

Something clicks into place.

When my Controller couldn't keep me preoccupied from my angsty teenage emotions with "responsible" behaviors like homework and algebra equations . . . another part of me stepped in out of the shadows.

My tiny, toothpick, swearing Inner Shadow.

The one who slashed the ink.

Who raged in secret.

Who silently screamed the f-bomb into her journal.

THE FLAMES OF THE SHADOW

Maybe you don't swear in the deep recesses of your mind. Maybe you don't secretly hate yourself or feel bitter toward God. Maybe you don't secretly harbor shame or resentment.

But I bet you feel things you're not proud of.

I'm guessing you've felt a spark of envy when you see that other mom's easy life—or what *looks* like ease from the outside.

I'm guessing you've felt a flicker of satisfaction when someone who always seems to get ahead finally hits a bump in the road.

Maybe you've secretly fantasized about walking away from it all—your marriage, your job, your life—to finally feel the warm glow of attention or relief.

I bet there are thoughts you bury before they ever see the light of day. I know because I have them too. And I want you to hear this:

It's okay.

I mean it. It's okay.

Not because I want you to linger there, but because underneath those shadowy thoughts is a wound that needs tending.

Everyone has a Shadow side. And you can either face it honestly . . . or pretend you don't have one and let it run roughshod over your life from the cave where you thought you buried it, deep inside.

THE SHADOW STANDS AT THE EDGE OF LONGING AND THE FANTASY OF RELIEF.

If your Inner Controller is like a tightly closed fist, the Shadow is more like a flame. Contained, a flame brings warmth, vitality, and life. Left unchecked, it rages into wildfire and scorches the earth, bringing damage and destruction in its wake. That is the reality of your Inner Shadow.

The Shadow stands at the edge of longing and the fantasy of relief. The ache beneath it—the flame—is not the problem. The danger comes when it's either ignored and left to spread unchecked or denied oxygen altogether and snuffed out. Left untended, it burns too hot. But when starved of air, you lose its warmth and vitality altogether. What your Shadow needs is *steady tending*—enough space to breathe, and the proper containment to keep it safe.

This is the work of becoming a secure soul in real time. And it requires the ongoing work of *soul tending*: the faithful, daily care that keeps the fire from becoming destructive in the first place. Soul tending is so much more than behavior management, duty, or even confession. It is soul *awareness*. It is attunement to the subtle movements within you.

The Shadow is a living, dynamic presence inside you. Your work, in partnership with God's Spirit, is to learn to recognize the first signs of heat—the shadowy feelings—not to quench them, but to tend them, respect their force, understand where they're coming from, and to *contain* them through the steady presence of Love. Love, after all, is the only force as strong as death (Song 8:6).

Because here's the thing: What becomes a destructive blaze *always* starts with a spark. And the way to keep that blaze from harming yourself, or others, is to learn to notice the sparks.

The Shadow's outbursts, her numbing, her fantasies, her simmering resentments—these are the sparks, the smoke, the first signs of heat. They are *bids for connection*, cries for compassion, pleas for a strong presence to help her tend the flame without burning you, or someone else, up.

When you don't recognize these bids, they can lead you down paths of destruction, scorching the inner terrain of your own soul, and burning through your connections with God and with others.

But when you learn to see them for what they are, you uncover the flicker of truth in the dark. Longings that, while painful, can also become embers of hope.

The Shadow holds that sacred fire of desire and ache. She reminds you when you're hurting, angry, or have been treated unjustly. That fire *has a place in your soul.* It's the crucible of your passion, your longings, and even your righteous anger.

And that flame needs you to tend to it, as an honored place within your soul. But it does not need to be allowed to blaze, unchecked, into what psychology calls harmful patterns, or what Scripture calls *sin*.

SHADOW OR SIN?

If you grew up in a culture that moralized every impulse, especially in faith settings, it may feel unsettling to acknowledge the Shadow's cries. Yet some of the wisest voices across time, including theologians, philosophers, and psychologists, agree on this: *Healing doesn't begin by exiling the Shadow.* Healing begins by first recognizing her ache.

Long before modern psychology gave us language for this, Scripture was already telling the story. Think of Zacchaeus, a man who was small in stature, despised, hiding behind the wealth he had gained at his neighbors' expense. Whatever his strategy had been for getting through life, it had cost him something, and he was cut off from real connection. And yet Jesus doesn't begin with condemnation. He begins with presence: "*I'm coming to your house.*" That kind of unearned welcome doesn't excuse harm, but it creates the safety that makes honesty possible. And from that place, Zacchaeus could finally choose repair (Luke 19:1–10).

Jesus saw more than his outer behaviors.
He saw the longing underneath:
to be seen,
to belong,
to be made whole.

His response wasn't condemnation—it was *presence*. And from that place of connection, he invited Zacchaeus into a new way of living.

Jesus models an *attachment-based approach to sin*. He addresses human brokenness through *secure presence*: holding honesty and compassion together in a way that *invites change through connection* rather than fear or shame. He doesn't minimize harmful patterns, but he looks beneath them to the vulnerable place within where love has lost its way.

JESUS MODELS AN *ATTACHMENT-BASED* APPROACH TO SIN.

Theologians like Augustine and Aquinas gave language to this insight, describing sin not primarily as rule breaking, but as disordered love—when an otherwise good longing for safety, worth, or belonging *bends back on itself and pulls us away from God and from others.*[1] Seen this way, sin is inseparable from woundedness. It so often grows out of it. And the antidote is not shame, but Love expressed through restoring connection.

Numerous contemporary psychologists and Christian spiritual writers have described this same relational dynamic of healing and repair that we see modeled in Jesus. Beloved priest and author Henri Nouwen often wrote about woundedness not as a barrier to God, but as the very place where Divine presence meets us.[2] And the good news, as professor and therapist Chuck DeGroat reminds us, is that "God shows up, not to fix, but with presence and compassion, offering questions bathed in curiosity."[3] Psychiatrist Curt Thompson similarly notes that transformation doesn't occur through shame or willpower, but *through being known and loved in the presence of another.*[4] Psychologist Hillary McBride echoes this wisdom, naming how shame and disconnection live not just in our thoughts, *but in our bodies.* Healing begins when those places are met with safety, tenderness, and relational care.[5]

TO DISREGARD EITHER REALITY—THE REALITY OF OUR HARMFUL PATTERNS *OR* THE TENDER PLACES BENEATH THEM—IS TO DO THE HUMAN SOUL A DISSERVICE.

Here's where this becomes tricky: What we often think of as sin takes root *in the soil of our vulnerabilities*, in the tender places where pain has not yet been met with secure, loving presence. In those hidden places, fear or hurt can distort genuine desire and pull us toward disconnection, self-destruction, and damage to relationships. To disregard either reality—the reality of our harmful patterns *or* the tender places beneath them—is to do the human soul a disservice.

In my own story, I've carried a harmful propensity toward self-evisceration and, at times, a persistent habit of comparison from those early teen years into adulthood. Long after things shifted socially, I still carried a deep internal sense of not being good enough. That insecurity didn't simply disappear when my circumstances changed.

And that insecurity gave rise to patterns I'm not proud of, patterns of harsh self-criticism, people-pleasing, and quiet resentments that didn't go away by simply telling myself to stop, praying my insecurity away, or repeating self-affirming mantras. I could fake confidence on the outside. But none of it touched the ache underneath.

Those patterns only began to change through this work of becoming a secure soul—the slow, honest work of *finding and connecting with the wounded places within*. As I recognized the cries of my young Inner Shadow, listened to her story, and met her not with contempt but with love, I began to form a secure attachment with this young part of my soul, an attachment rooted not in fixing or managing her, but in presence and care. And from that place, these patterns began to change.

THOSE PATTERNS ONLY BEGAN TO CHANGE THROUGH THIS WORK OF BECOMING A SECURE SOUL—THE SLOW, HONEST WORK OF *FINDING AND CONNECTING WITH THE WOUNDED PLACES WITHIN*.

This distinction matters: *These tender places within you*

are not the problem. They are *sacred soil* where your longing to be loved, to be safe, and to belong first took root.

Think of the Shadow as the signal that there is a wound—a vital sign that something within has been hurt. The wound isn't the danger. But when the Shadow's signals are minimized, spiritually bypassed, or left untended, infection can set in, spreading harm both inwardly and outwardly.

Healing begins when you learn to distinguish between the two: the ache at the root and the harmful patterns that grew up around it. What the aching part of you needs is loving presence. It needs the curiosity, compassion, and yes, containment we all need in order to heal and flourish.

SECURE ATTACHMENT IS NEITHER SUPPRESSION NOR INDULGENCE. SECURE ATTACHMENT IS *PRESENCE*.

This Shadow part of your soul doesn't need to be silenced or shamed. She needs to be *shepherded*. She needs to know there's a presence strong enough to hold her big feelings, her uncensored thoughts, and the pain she's been holding alone—the pain she learned no one else could, or would, hold.

Because when her pain is finally, and consistently, met with loving presence, she no longer drives your life from the margins. She becomes, instead, a source of vitality, truthfulness, and a deeply rooted inner security.

And from that place, you can begin to take brave, wise actions—actions that honor both your longing *and* your integrity.

CONTAINING THE FLAME

In moments of vulnerability, we face a quiet but consequential choice: to turn toward Love, or to reach for something else that promises a quick hit of relief.

We see this dynamic played out in the garden when Adam and Eve were tempted precisely at the place of their vulnerability and chose disconnection (Gen. 3:1–7). And we see it again in the wilderness, when Jesus faced hunger, weariness, and loneliness (Matt. 4:1–11). He, too, was tempted at the very place of his longing. Yet he made a different choice. He recognized the ache and turned toward his Father, anchoring himself in Love.

We don't tend to hold this tension well in our culture—the tension between our ache and the agency we possess. In many religious communities, we're taught to clamp down on painful or uncomfortable feelings with willpower, control, or even shame. On the other hand, therapy sound bites, especially on social media, can make validation sound like the whole goal, without the slower work of discernment, truth-telling, and wise action.

TRUST CREATES THE SAFETY THAT MAKES AGENCY POSSIBLE.

But secure attachment is neither suppression nor indulgence.

Secure attachment is *presence.*

And presence holds with compassion and containment.

Compassion, not indulgence.

Containment, not control.

Over time, compassion and containment create the conditions for choice, for what psychology calls agency, and what Scripture calls wisdom. When your inner world is held with care, you're no longer reacting on autopilot. You regain the capacity to pause, to notice what is stirring within you, and to *choose connection instead of compulsion.*

This kind of choosing doesn't emerge from willpower, shame, or indulgence. It emerges from *safety.* From staying present with what's happening inside long enough for wisdom to break through.

Imagine holding a child in the middle of a tantrum. She's angry, sobbing, and overwhelmed by frustration. You don't shame her. You don't abandon her. *You hold her.*

What she needs most is presence. Someone who'll bear witness to her pain, her anger, her fear, and say: *I see you. You're not too much for me. I'll stay with you.*

Eventually, the tears quiet. She feels safe, and her nervous system settles. She begins to trust again, not only her bond with you, but also the bond within herself.

Trust creates the safety that makes agency possible.

As trust returns, her thinking mind comes back online, restoring her ability to pause, reflect, and choose with wisdom.

Only then can you ask the deeper questions together:

What do we do about this bully?

This betrayal?

This rejection?

This heartache?

This injustice?

Brave actions begin to take shape from a steady, confident

place inside. A place where courage and wisdom are finally able to connect.

Here's what is true: *That young child—the one who sometimes comes undone in pain—still lives within you.*

And when she is met with compassion and containment, her pain becomes information. *It becomes fuel for brave, wise action.*

Envy may reveal a longing for something good and life-giving.

Resentment may uncover a part of you longing to be seen and valued.

Pining after what isn't yours may expose an ache for connection and belonging.

Secrecy may point to a fear that honesty will cost you love.

What once felt shameful is so often an attachment need in disguise.

These shadowy responses are not evidence that something is wrong with you—they are invitations. Invitations to slow down. To listen. To recognize the Shadow and gently help her return to Love.

And that's what I finally began to do with my own swearing Inner Shadow.

CONNECTING WITH YOUR INNER SHADOW

I come back to that young Inner Shadow, the one scratching the f-word into her journal. The one who still carries the quick flare of resentment, the tiny, urgent songs of "not enough."

I lean in close and whisper, *I'm here with you.*

And like a shift in the light she takes shape: real, trembling, no longer alone. She lets me into the storm she's been carrying.

It's not fair, she sobs. *I hate how invisible I am. I'll never be good enough.*

I want to talk her out of these feelings, to reroute that old neural pathway of insecurity and comparison right there where it first formed. But she doesn't need my words. She doesn't need my Inner Controller to frantically push her away.

She needs my *presence.*

She needs me to *stay with her* while she cries. To hold her shame without fixing it.

So I stay. Until she cries herself to sleep and I can almost feel her presence in my arms.

She's starting to trust me. And I want to be worthy of that trust.

But my adult self also feels unsure how best to help her. So while she rests, I shift my attention toward God. My eyes are wide, and my heart is tender with that familiar, parental-like sense of helplessness. *I want to help her, God. I'm not sure what to do.*

God, how do you see this young shadowy part of my soul? She needs me. And I need you.

And I begin to *mediate* on her behalf. In my mind's eye, I cradle her tiny, sleeping, toothpick body in the arms of my soul and hold her up to him.

I tell God more about her story, sort of like how I might

update my husband about something I've become aware of in one of our kids: small, aching details offered in the quiet of love.

Did you know how much she hated herself back then, pressing her pen so hard she ripped the page?

Did you see her savoring those secret Sweet Valley High *books when she was alone?*

Were you there, God, when she stood in front of the mirror, picking herself apart?

Did you see the swirling fantasies of crushes and comparisons, the longing she didn't know how to hold?

God, do you know this part of me? The one who lived in the shadows for so long? Do you know the way I still struggle at times with scarcity, smallness, and comparison? The way I can eviscerate myself?

As I share her story with God, I realize I'm no longer carrying this aching part of me alone. *What was an inner place of loneliness is now bathed in loving presence.*

I don't sense tidy answers, only a nearness that *fills my soul.*

It's as if God's presence is wrapping us both in Love—the young girl who still lives inside of me, and the adult self who so deeply wants to heal.

God's love is traveling across time and space, reaching back to that very place where I once felt so bereft.

Meeting us in the very place where the pain first entered in. Awakening something she could not then trust—that she was *always* seen, always held, always beloved, even there in her tiny, toothpick body. And at the same time, awakening me to the depth of that same truth today.

I am so deeply aware of God's presence, a God who *longs to reclaim every part of us*.

A God who doesn't always keep us from harm, but who always comes to meet us in the ache.

A God who doesn't just talk about love, but who *embodies* it.

A God who doesn't chastise, lecture, or criticize, but simply *stays with us*.

A God who is unafraid of our rage, unshaken by our sorrow.

I sense a Love I have long known about but not always felt deep within. A Love big enough to hold the tender nuances of my own story, and also the heavier pain carried by so many others.

I think about the adjudicated teens I worked with at a correctional school just out of college—how so much of their behavior grew from deep attachment wounds and unresolved trauma. And how, over time, the steady, loving presence of therapists and teachers began to draw out a softness, a tenderness, an openness to change.

I think about the paroled men and women my husband and I met with weekly for over a decade as we studied Scripture and asked hard questions together. How their addiction-fueled choices were so often rooted in deep, early wounds. So many of them could point to a specific moment when a younger version of themselves tried to quiet pain too big to name. And I think of what we learned in that room: not to push to solve or explain, but to honor the story. How bearing witness brought forth connectedness again and again.

And I begin to see more clearly that what brings healing *is always presence.*

Our shadow selves emerge at the intersection of real pain and our clumsy, often costly, attempts to find relief. And only God is truly big enough, wise enough, tender enough to meet us in that fragile space where heartache meets the longing for escape.

And yet God so often meets us there through ordinary means: through parents and teachers, therapists and pastors, grandparents and steady friends, through the imperfect, fumbling faithfulness of human love. And sometimes he meets us through other quiet graces.

I think back to myself as a young teenager, driving toward the mountain with the windows down, blasting '80s hair bands. How the car became a container. The mountain, a towering attachment figure, strong enough to hold my pain. How the music itself became a cry of the Shadow, rising from the depths of my being.

I turn back to where this young Shadow part of me is slowly waking up, still held in the arms of my soul. And I speak the words I wish I could have heard back then, words I've helped others learn to say.

Words my own soul needs to receive even now, in its deepest, darkest corners.

I see you.

I know how hard it has been to live in this body and feel so alone inside it. I want to help you feel safe here—with me and with God.

Your body isn't a problem to fix. She's growing. She's trying. She is worthy of care and love.

When you feel shame, I want you to let me in. I can't promise to take away everything that hurts. But I can promise this: I will not leave you.

And as you stay close to me, and we stay close to God, I promise you'll grow into someone whole. Someone strong. Someone kind. Someone beautiful.

You don't have to do this alone anymore. Will you stay connected with me?

I'm struck by how deeply she trusts me and how calm she feels in my strength. She doesn't need to be fixed. She needs the steadiness of my presence.

This is how we begin to bring the Shadow into the light—not to shame her, not to cajole her into being different, but to first and foremost *connect* with her at the place where the wound was formed.

Because here's what I didn't understand back then, or for the next few decades of my adult life: The Shadow doesn't disappear when you suppress her.

She goes underground. She hides in silence, in shame, in distrust. In bitter resentments, self-loathing, and comparisons. You can manage her for a while. But she's still there.

I didn't realize it, at least *not fully*, until I met her again on that late-night prayer walk through London.

When I felt a distinct sense of her presence still inside me: *I don't like God very much.*

It was the voice of this deeply feeling Inner Shadow, seeking connection all along.

Recognize: *I'm hurting.*

Return: *I am loved. Even here.*

CHAPTER 6

TEND A DIVIDED SOUL

The Controller and the Shadow may look like opposites. One powers you up, helping you stay focused, put-together, sleeves rolled up to the elbow. The other powers you down, numbing you out with snacks or screens, or retreating into the dark caves of resentment and bitterness.

The Controller takes charge so you won't get hurt again. She's held you together, tried to make you presentable, managed your image, and worked to ensure that you appear good, responsible, and worthy. She is all about order, performance, and holding things in line. But she was never meant to carry the whole weight. She needs to know *you* are the adult in your soul, and that God is the One she can *always* lean on.

The Shadow carries the more raw, less "socially acceptable" passions. She's held the resentment, jealousy, disappointment, and anger—even anger toward God. She is seeking outlets for the fiery, passionate, and often uncomfortable feelings you've so often tried to push out of sight. Without care, she can react in ways that wound both you and others. She needs to know you are strong enough to stay with her big feelings and still hold her safe. That God does not shy away from her sparks but stays with her in the fire. And that together, you'll help her find a truer way.

When these two parts both try to take the lead, your soul gets divided. The Controller tightens her grip, pushing you harder to maintain control, while the Shadow resists, simmering with frustration beneath the surface. One pushes for perfection and order; the other rebels against it. It's a tug-of-war between order and chaos, between appearing fine and feeling all the things you actually feel. The result is exhaustion—a life lived from tension rather than a deep-seated trust.

And that's exactly what happened to me before I learned about this work of becoming a secure soul. There came a point when the tension inside me snapped. The Controller and the Shadow were locked in their silent war until something finally broke.

THE DAY MY SOUL SPLIT OPEN

I can see her even now. She's thirty years old, hair pulled back in a ponytail, flannel shirt draped over the skinny jeans of the early 2000s. Her head is bent toward the glow of a laptop, shoulders hunched up, fingers flying as she perfects an essay on moral psychology for graduate school.

She. Cannot. Stop. Perfecting.

By this time in my life, I am completely blended with my Inner Controller—the part of me who works so hard to be respectable to the outside world. She has been working overtime for more than a decade to keep me safe. Only now, she's traded algebra books for a laptop, psychology texts, and graduate-level research papers.

She's hunched over inside a small, sunlit apartment whose bare walls don't even register to her. She's never been one to decorate. Completely cut off from her body, she's desperate to outwork the geyser of unacknowledged pain, loneliness, and fear about to take her over.

Her mantra for over a decade has been: *Don't complain. Help others.* And she has absolutely no idea that this mantra is about to undo her.

Outwardly, this young Controller was terrifyingly productive. I was working full-time while simultaneously carrying a full course load in psychology and theology, writing papers that moved my professors by day and leading support groups for women with eating disorders by night. I was also the reliable friend in my off time, always showing up. I counted over a dozen bridesmaid dresses in my closet, having stood up at as many weddings. As one by one my friends left to launch their new lives, I didn't stop to notice how my own life was growing smaller and smaller.

Meanwhile, my family was unraveling. My sister's divorce had opened a painful rift between my parents and her, my three beloved attachment figures. As the youngest, it felt like I was the child caught in the middle of their growing divide. Night after night, I talked to each one of them on the phone translating, smoothing, and peacekeeping, doing everything I could to keep my family from breaking apart. I thought I was helping them, unaware that I was actually desperately trying to keep my own self together.

Inwardly, I was completely cut off. My Inner Shadow was walled away by well-intentioned but misguided tactics. The Controller had declared her shadowy feelings—anger, resentment, loneliness—off-limits. *It's sinful to feel angry. You should be grateful. You shouldn't need more than what you have.* So I resorted to escape. I'd watch *You've Got Mail* on repeat, disappearing into someone else's story, living vicariously through fantasies of connection. I'd wander the streets of my neighborhood alone, staring into the windows of sparkling restaurants filled with laughing couples and families, craving a sense of joy and togetherness I couldn't find a way to make my own. Or I'd bury the ache in a deep-fried grilled cheese sandwich, each savory bite a quiet rebellion against all the "shoulds."

And then came the day I remember so vividly: The sunlight spills onto the bare white walls of my apartment.

It should feel warm. Instead, it only illuminates the emptiness.

The cursor on my laptop blinks. My mind races. I am working overtime to stay ahead of the pain. Revising, revising, revising.

And then, suddenly, I reach the end. I can't find another word to change or fix.

The paper is finished. The laptop is closed.

A moment of utter silence. I am confused. My mind is like a blinking checkout light in the grocery store: "System processing," only nothing is happening.

I feel an emptiness I can't explain.

I keep reaching for something to do, scanning my mental Rolodex for someone to help—but it's not working.

For the first time in a year, I have a moment to myself, with nothing to accomplish and no one to save.

And in that sudden, breathless quiet of this empty room—my paper turned in, a day off from work, hands empty, no project or person to fix—the dam inside me bursts. The walls of my inner soul mountain collapse all at once, and a silent scream erupts from every cell in my body:

I'm. Not. Fine.

Only it doesn't come out in words. It erupts as a full-body panic attack—a crushing, disorienting wave of anger and terror flooding my chest, my throat, my whole being.

I literally feel like I'm going to die. I can't stand. I can't think straight. My psychologist brain is useless. I *know* about panic attacks. This knowledge does not help me.

I call my dad, two thousand miles away. "Dad, I feel like I'm going to die. I don't know what to do." His voice is quiet, uncertain. "We better get you to the emergency room."

But I'm alone. There's no one to drive me. Somehow, I'll have to get there myself. As I fumble for my keys, I remember my friend Stacy, a therapist colleague I've been co-leading eating disorder groups with.

"Stacy," I gasp into the phone. "I'm not okay. I think I'm having a panic attack."

"Are you safe to drive?" she asks. "I can't leave; I've got kids here."

"I think so."

"Then stay on the phone with me," she says. "Drive to my house."

Somehow, with Stacy's voice in my ear, I manage to drive the short distance to her house. She's outside waiting, surrounded by four kids of her own and half the neighborhood swirling around her. I stumble out of the car, and she runs to meet me, catching me as I fall into her arms.

Every emotion I've buried for years pours out all at once. Behind me, the car is still running with the keys locked inside. Neither of us cares.

I'm not one to cry with other people. I'm the one who holds others as they cry. But here I am—a thirty-year-old woman, standing in the middle of a cul-de-sac, sobbing into my colleague's arms while the neighborhood kids laugh and play all around us.

Stacy takes me into her home, where her young son moves out of his bedroom and I move in—sleeping beneath his *Star Wars* posters for the next week—so I don't have to be alone anymore.

WHEN PARTS OF YOU TAKE OVER

It's one thing to hide in your books as a teenager. It's another to keep hiding there as an adult.

It's one thing to sneak romance novels as a girl. It's

another to live inside a fantasy world rather than risk real love in your adult life.

This was my soul at thirty. My Controller kept me tightly wrapped up in studies and books, producing the perfect paper, being the good daughter, the low-maintenance friend. She didn't even know there was another way. And when she faltered, my Shadow stepped in with grilled cheese sandwiches, daydreams of love, and fantasies of comfort.

For a while, the system worked.

Until it didn't.

Maybe you've been there too. Maybe you haven't collapsed into panic attacks, but you've had moments when your world seemed to fall apart. When someone betrayed you. When you couldn't find your way out of a toxic relationship. When anxiety (or the need to escape from it) got the best of you.

When these inner parts of your soul don't receive compassion and containment, they grow too strong in your soul. They take on roles they were never meant to carry, developing survival strategies that eventually *wound* the very soul they're trying to keep safe.

Sometimes your Inner Controller takes over, as mine did—proving, perfecting, and pleasing—determined to hold it all together.

- Maybe your Controller keeps you parenting in overdrive—constantly correcting, fixing, and second-guessing. You can't figure out how to "let go."
- Maybe she drives you to perform—taking on projects, working late, proving yourself again and again. You're exhausted, but you can't stop.

- Maybe she urges you toward perfectionism—replaying conversations, editing emails five times, making sure nothing slips through the cracks. You wish you could rest, but you can't.
- Maybe your Controller pushes you to please everyone—smoothing over every conflict and saying yes when you're exhausted. You can't figure out why you still feel so alone.

Other times, the Shadow steps in to soothe the ache that follows. She numbs, distracts, and quietly resents, determined to survive the pressure.

- Maybe your Shadow sneaks in late at night—scrolling, snacking, or collapsing in front of the TV, drowning out the noise in the flicker of distraction.
- Maybe she rebels with comfort eating, overspending, or procrastination. Letting out your exhaustion in a silent cry of *I deserve this!*
- Maybe she retreats into fantasy—romance novels, pornography, or daydreams of a different life, indulging a genuine longing with a soul-numbing substitute.
- Maybe she develops a full-blown addiction.

And typically, these two parts of your soul operate in tandem. They push and pull against each other, creating an internal tug-of-war that keeps your soul spinning.

- Your Controller says yes to everyone; your Shadow resents it.
- Your Controller keeps you performing; your Shadow dreams of disappearing.
- Your Controller tries to hold it all together; your Shadow plans her escape.

The Controller whispers, *It's not safe to stop.*

The Shadow protests, *I can't keep going like this.*

Your soul becomes divided, locked in a battle between the Controller's hum of urgency and the Shadow's reflex to escape. All the while, there is *no space for the ache underneath.*

THIS IS THE BID OF A DIVIDED SOUL: ONE PART POWERING UP TO CONTROL, ANOTHER POWERING DOWN TO ESCAPE.

This is the bid of a divided soul: one part powering up to control, another powering down to escape. Both trying, in their own way, to keep you safe.

A soul desperately in need of attunement, compassion, and loving presence.

POLARIZATIONS

This back-and-forth inside your soul—shifting from powering up to powering down—is something we all do on some level. On any given day, you might work hard, and then choose to take a break by watching a favorite sitcom at night.

A healthy soul recognizes the natural rhythms of work and rest, of diligence and play.

But in a healthy soul, you're *aware* of these choices. Let's say you had a rough day at work. Your boss criticized a project you poured yourself into. You're tired and don't want to think about it, let alone try to explain what happened to your spouse.

A HEALTHY SOUL RECOGNIZES THE NATURAL RHYTHMS OF WORK AND REST, OF DILIGENCE AND PLAY.

Your inner monologue might sound like this: *I'm going to pour myself a glass of wine and curl up with a three-hour Netflix binge. I know there's a lot I need to process, but tonight I just need a break. I'll come back to what happened at work in the morning.*

And the next morning, you do just that. You get up, make some coffee, take a deep breath, and begin to reengage with what happened. You journal. You talk it through with a friend or your spouse. You reflect on what you'll do next.

You let your mind and body rest when they need to, without retreating into avoidance or escapism. And when it's time, you do the work you need to do. You honor the rhythm of your soul, pacing yourself as you move between effort and care.

But sometimes this rhythm gets off beat. You push through when you should pause. Or you distract yourself when you really need to reflect. You lose touch with the gentle pacing of a healthy soul. And when this gets extreme, it becomes what psychologists call a polarization.[1]

A polarization occurs when these parts of your inner

world take extreme, opposing roles. What was meant to be a rhythm becomes an *inner dissonance*: a harsh back-and-forth between parts of you that are both trying to help but have forgotten how to work together.

And the result is a battle inside your own soul.

- One part admonishes you about how much work you have to do. Another zones out on a Netflix bender.
- One part insists you must keep pleasing someone who hurts you. Another simmers with resentment and vents to your friends.
- One part pushes you to eat perfectly and never touch a processed particle. Another rebels with late-night snacks or secret binges.

These inner standoffs keep your soul locked in opposition. Instead of working together, parts of you fight for control. And the result is *more* tension inside your soul.

When parts battle, your nervous system reacts. Your Inner Controller launches into fight mode. Your Inner Shadow flees into flight. The amygdala and brain stem go on high alert, stress hormones rise, and it becomes even harder to access the calm, creative center of your soul—the very qualities you actually need.

The self-defeating nature of the polarized soul is a vivid example of Newton's third law of motion: For every action, there is an equal and opposite reaction.

The harder your Inner Controller digs in, the harder your Inner Shadow pushes back.

Like the apostle Paul, you can't figure out why you don't

do the things you want to do (Rom. 7:15). And most of us, at least here in the West, tend to blame our Inner Shadow:

What's wrong with you? Why can't you be more disciplined? your Inner Controller yells.

But that yelling doesn't help. The Shadow doubles down.

And the battle wages on.

The inner calm you need most gets blocked, taking courage, clarity, and wisdom with it.

You end up working *against yourself.*

The results aren't good. You feel emotional tension, dissonance, exhaustion, and a sense of being stuck. And you're cut off from the deeper needs inside your soul.

It's like when two parents are fighting over how best to care for their child. In the tension of their argument, the child—the very one they're trying to protect—ends up being ignored!

The truth is: Neither part has it quite right. And neither one is entirely wrong. But they'll never get to where your soul needs to be while they're fighting with each other.

Your job is not to choose between them.

Instead, it's to take a deep breath and recognize:

I'm divided.

I'm conflicted.

I'm fighting within myself.

And sometimes, your soul simply rises up and says, *Enough!*

That's what happened to me.

I couldn't recognize the dissonance inside. And so my soul did what my mind could not—it split me open. It brought me to my knees, down to the place of surrender we often discover only at the end of ourselves.

THE GIFT OF THE BREAKDOWN

Moving into a little boy's room in my friend's already overcrowded house at thirty was my rock bottom, the place where I couldn't pretend anymore. I was anxious, sleepless, and *dependent* on someone else.

It was also the beginning of rebirth.

I needed to stop running from the ache within my soul. I needed to finally start listening to it.

Because even in that low point, in the collapse of all I thought I was building, something sacred was taking root.

A new way of being with—and tending to—my soul.

This new way took root slowly, but persistently, in small moments I barely knew how to name, as I began to *recognize* my disconnection and *return* to Love. As I began to reach for the tethers that Love sent, in ways I'd never done before.

It took root as I let Stacy walk with me into a doctor's office, where my Inner Shadow finally whispered aloud to another human what she had been feeling down deep inside: "I don't know how to stop the pain."

The doctor asked with care, "Are you going to hurt yourself?"

"No. I just don't know how to make the pain stop." And then, moved by his kindness, a flicker of levity: "It might help if I stop reading existential philosophers for a while."

It took root as the anti-anxiety medication he prescribed helped me sleep beneath those *Star Wars* posters, medication that didn't heal my soul but helped me regain my footing.

It took root as I sat with Stacy over coffee and, for the first time, tried to explain the rift within my family. And how she named the pattern *triangulation*, a term I had studied but had never thought to apply to my own experience. How the name fit, unlocking deeper healing.

It took root as my family and friends, who I finally started to let in, listened and honored and cared.

It took root as I set boundaries with my Inner Controller, not always lovingly back then, but still necessary.

No more school. No more books—at least not for a while. I took an incomplete for the quarter that stretched into three years off. Instead, I took a job tutoring children. Each day I helped middle school students with their algebra homework, soaking in their giggles and keeping them entertained. One parent told me, "I've never heard so much laughter during a tutoring session." Slowly, my Inner Controller learned to play again.

It took root as I began to recognize the needs of my Inner Shadow. Instead of resorting to fantasy in isolation, I signed up for an acting class. Every Tuesday night, under the stage lights and alongside real scene partners, I gave my soul permission to speak. I learned to express anger, anguish, and desire through the voices of fictional characters.

And to my surprise, my classmates *loved* this side of me, delighted as they watched this so-called "good girl" come alive, even as a villain. For my Shadow, it was pure joy and also relief, as she discovered a creative outlet for emotions she had long learned to hide.

The shift didn't happen overnight. But it happened slowly, gently, and truly as I learned to tend the terrain of my inner soul mountain.

And over time, I began to notice something surprising:

These small acts of tuning in to my own ache, to God, and to my longing for connection began to form something stronger than I expected.

They formed a kind of inner web of trust. A sacred holding place. A deep security within.

An inner strength and sense of connectedness that didn't depend on my circumstances or on other people—but did now include them.

Slowly the two warring sides of my soul began to work together. They began to find balance and even a glimpse of harmony.

They learned to share responsibility instead of fighting for control. To this day, I have never again experienced the same level of anxiety or loneliness I once knew back then.

And in the space that opened up between their loosening grips, a voice that had always been there finally had room to be heard.

A tender, living part of me—awake, aware, and quietly present at the center.

One who had long carried both delight and ache. Wonder and need. Longing and hope.

And now, at last, her voice could be heard.

The one whispering:

I need love too.

Recognize: *I'm coming undone.*

Return: *I am loved, even here.*

CHAPTER 7

FIND THE YOUNG ONE INSIDE

Neither your Inner Controller nor your Inner Shadow is out to ruin you. Both are trying to help you survive. They clash because they disagree on *how* to help. It's like having two loyal guardians inside, each with a plan, each convinced it's right. But in the tug-of-war, they miss a quieter voice.

Because beneath their noise and conflict lies something far more tender and just as alive.

It's the deepest place within your soul mountain. The place where wonder still lives and where the ache of disconnection first took root.

Where trust is still possible—and where you've most needed care.

Where joy bubbles up—and where pain left its mark.

This is the tender place inside your soul that the Controller and the Shadow would do anything to protect. Not because it's weak, but because it's precious.

It is the Young One inside of you.

The Young One is the soft, beating center beneath all your adult armor. The part of you who carries unguarded longing and tenderness, curiosity and playful innocence, wonder and, yes, the capacity to be wounded. She is the childlike heart at the center of your soul.[1]

More than anything, she needs to know she is safe.

That she is connected.

That she is cherished.

And as your Controller and your Shadow begin to trust that *you* are here to notice, to care, and to *stay*, something shifts. Their urgency eases. Their noise softens. Space opens.

You begin to sense the Young One's presence within.

THE YOUNG ONE IS THE SOFT, BEATING CENTER BENEATH ALL YOUR ADULT ARMOR.

Sometimes her presence shows up as need. And sometimes it shows up as wisdom.

Because she isn't only the one in need of rescue. *She's also the one who remembers the way back to Love.*

THE ONE IN NEED OF RESCUE

I drop my two sweet, elderly doodles off at the groomer's, the same place my mom and I brought our dogs when I was a child. Across the street looms my old red-brick middle school, the place where my locker mate's boyfriend once mocked me, where I felt unseen, where my body felt like a burden.

This morning, in my current life, kids swarm outside the building, backpacks slung over small shoulders. As I watch them, I feel that familiar flash of a rescuing impulse. An urge rises up within me to walk into the crowd, gather every single one of these middle-school children up, and *rescue them*.

Rescue them from what? I'm not sure. It's not logical. Just an incredibly powerful feeling.

I used to feel this often. At the movies. At the gym. Anywhere I saw children gathering in social groups. A deep ache would well up inside me, followed by a fierce desire to save them from some impending doom.

It's an understandable instinct in some ways, one I've seen in so many of my clients over these past two decades.

But it's also dangerous. Because the part of me that wants to rescue is *very* young. And she's led me into a fair amount of relational quicksand.

Not everyone needs—or wants—to be rescued.

Not everyone needs *me* to be the one rescuing them.

Over time, I have learned that this urgency to save other people is often a disguised plea for rescue coming from a part of myself. And so, as I notice this urgency now, I pause, as I've learned to do, and I ask God to show me more about where this feeling is coming from.

Almost instantly, I sense a much younger version of me, a brown-eyed girl sporting the Dorothy Hamill haircut of the early '80s, in the plaid brown gingham dress her mom made for her. She's in a different classroom now—second grade. Sun streams through square windows onto lined-up desks, illuminating the paradox of what feels like a familiar sort of loneliness.

She's seated in the row closest to the door, second from the back, farthest from the teacher, whose desk is all the way on the opposite corner of the room.

Sitting just behind her is a boy who makes her feel uneasy. He's giant in her mind, like a grown man, the kind of kid who's always in trouble with the teacher. And she can feel something heavy around him, something she doesn't know how to name, only how to sense.

At first, I wonder if this boy scares her. But then I realize: It's not exactly fear. It's worry, mixed with a little confusion. Worry about what he carries. Confusion about how her presence might affect him.

She has to pass her spelling test back to him to be graded, and she doesn't like it. Sometimes the papers go the other way, and she ends up grading his. He struggles. And sometimes, almost without even deciding to, she nudges an answer in his favor, just a little, so he won't fail.

And now she knows he's about to see that she doesn't struggle in the same way, and that awareness stirs up a confusing heat in her chest—something my adult self can only name as embarrassment, maybe even *shame*.

She is seven—old enough to feel empathy and social discomfort, yet too young to know what to do with it.

Other kids tease him. She notices.

Come to think of it, she notices a lot.

She notices the boy and the kids who are mean to him.

She notices the other girls, but she doesn't know how to reach them.

She notices the unease that keeps her planted in her seat, unsure what to do with her hands, her words, herself.

She was scanning the room, even then—awake, attuned, and also *alone* with all she took in.

No one knew how she would carry this boy, and others like him, over the coming years. How that mixture of worry, confusion, and shame would settle into her body. Until now, when I'm finally slowing down long enough to sit with her and notice her ache.

Nothing remarkable happens in that classroom.

Nothing anyone would think to point to or explain.

Only unmirrored worry. And loneliness. The kind that forms not because something bad happened but because something essential didn't get seen.

And at the edge of this memory, something profound is taking shape: *Feelings have arrived but do not yet know where to go.*

It took me a long time to figure out why the memory of that sunlit classroom, and the boy sitting behind me, stayed with me. But I've learned that when a memory lingers, it's wise to pay attention. These memories don't only point us to where the ache of disconnection was first felt; they reveal where something important is being born.

THE POWER OF MEMORY

As an adult, you carry every prior version of yourself through the power of memory. You carry the baby who once cried when you were hungry or uncomfortable. You carry the child who braved the first day of kindergarten and survived fifth grade. You carry the teen who stumbled through high school, trying to make sense of parents, siblings, teachers, and peers. These younger versions of you don't disappear; they live on inside you, shaping how you feel, react, and relate in the present day.

So when an early memory surfaces—even when you can't figure out why, and even when it feels insignificant—pay attention. That's not random. Sometimes a memory surfaces like a breadcrumb pointing toward a trail.

Our brains are wired for survival. When something feels threatening—whether it's a harsh word, a public humiliation, a physical danger—or simply when something formative or emotionally significant happens, the brain tags that moment as important. The nervous system ramps up, and those memories can get stored with unusual vividness . . . or in fragments that return later.

In other words, your brain takes a kind of snapshot: *Pay attention. Something happened here*. That's why you may not remember what you had for lunch last Tuesday, but you can recall in vivid detail the classroom where you were humiliated, the expression on someone's face when you felt rejected, or the moment you realized you were alone with something you didn't know how to carry.

And here's how this relates to this work of becoming a secure soul: Memory is the trail that leads you back to the parts of your soul still in need of your care. Not just to the moment itself, but to the younger version of you who lived it.

One way to understand this is through what psychiatrist Dan Siegel calls neural integration, and what neuroscience more broadly calls memory reconsolidation. When you revisit a memory with intention and care, especially when you can stay present to it in a new way, your brain doesn't simply replay it like a recording. Instead, the memory becomes pliable. In other words, it becomes open to being reshaped.[2]

This means that, over time, you can begin to change how your brain stores and responds to a painful experience. Rather than piling on new bandages to cover the wound, you can tend to it directly by acknowledging what happened, honoring the pain, and creating new pathways for healing. You can gently tend to the place in your soul where the wound first formed. (Please note: If your early experiences include abuse, violence, or overwhelming trauma, this work is not meant to be done alone. The presence of a wise, trained professional matters.)

MEMORY IS THE TRAIL THAT LEADS YOU BACK TO THE PARTS OF YOUR SOUL STILL IN NEED OF YOUR CARE.

When you return to these memories, you are tending an attachment wound through the power of loving presence. You're forming new pathways, and new ways of responding, right where the old ones first formed.

Scripture affirms this mystery too. God's healing presence is not bound by time or space. As the psalmist said, "Where can I go from your Spirit? Where can I flee from your presence?" (Ps. 139:7). When you return prayerfully to a past moment of loneliness, fear, or pain, you can connect with God in the place where the wound first took root. It doesn't erase what happened, but God's healing presence can transform the way what happened lives in you.

You can't rewrite history. But you can rewrite the story your soul carries about that history. What that means is that you can:

- Honor the truth of what happened, acknowledging that it mattered.
- Connect with God's healing presence in the places that still hurt.
- Move forward with intention, grounded in the agency you have today.

You can meet that younger version of yourself with the compassion, curiosity, and containment she didn't receive at the time. You can let her know:

I see what you went through.

I know what happened.

I'm here with you now.

You don't have to hold this alone anymore.

GOD'S HEALING PRESENCE IS NOT BOUND BY TIME OR SPACE.

It is never too late to change the story you carry.

WHEN A PART OF YOU GETS STUCK

As I reconnect with that seven-year-old girl in the sunny classroom with the "scary" boy who wasn't really scary, I ask God to help me understand why this memory is so deeply etched in my soul. To help me understand *her*, this Young One who still lives in me.

And slowly, another layer of that year comes back to me. I remember more of what was happening *around me*.

My older sister was being shunned by her entire fourth-grade class. This was before anti-bullying was a thing. Teachers were kind, but they didn't intervene. For months, several girls from our own neighborhood led the others to stop speaking to her. No friends at recess, no one to sit with at lunch.

IT IS NEVER TOO LATE TO CHANGE THE STORY YOU CARRY.

As I sit with this Young One now, I begin to wonder—not about my sister, whose story I've carried for years, or about the bullies whose faces I remember, but about *her*. About the seven-year-old who was taking all of this in.

Memories return not as a story, but as flashes. She projects details to me like an old movie projector showing shadowy images on a wall.

My mom, anxiously talking with someone on the phone, trying to figure out what to do.

The neighborhood girls—the ones who wouldn't speak to my sister—blithely playing tetherball on our pole while we watched from inside.

The boy in my classroom—always in trouble, older than his years—sitting just behind me.

The images are mostly focused on others. Very little about her.

And I think about how, even now, when I feel out of sorts, my attention still moves outward. I'll turn to my husband (or even our dogs) and ask, "Are you okay?"

It's taken us both years to realize that when I compulsively check on him, nine times out of ten what I'm really saying is:

"*I'm* not okay. *I* need reassurance. *I'm* feeling scared, lonely, or confused."

And that's when it clicks: This is where it started.

Where the gift of empathy also became a wound.

Where I learned to rely on taking in the data of other people's pain—without, at the same time, learning how to know my own.

Where I learned that my role was to observe. To manage. To attune outwardly.

Where I learned to track everyone else—and lost track of me.

And what I notice now as I stay with her is that, beneath all that observing, *she* is alone.

And without someone to help her understand that what was happening around her was also leaving its mark on *her*, other parts stepped in.

My Controller focused on homework and on trying to rescue others. My Shadow learned to self-soothe through fantasy and escape. And quietly, this Young One carried the burden of feeling invisible. Alone. Unseen.

The truth is, this Young One carried both a gift and a burden. Her sensitivity—this quality that would one day become empathy—was beautiful. But it also needed tending, compassion and loving *containment*.

And without someone to help me understand what was happening around me, as well as how it also impacted me, other parts of me stepped in.

I focused on my homework. I stayed out of the way. I minimized my own needs. And quietly, I formed an idea about love and connection: *I am the one who sees others. I am the one who helps. I am the one who rescues.*

What this Young One needed wasn't more responsibility. What this little girl needed was for someone to notice what *she* carried, her own ache beneath all the watching.

She, too, was lonely.

She, too, needed care.

THE HIDDEN BURDEN OF THE YOUNG ONE

Over the years, I have seen similar burdens carried by the Young One in many different people. The wounds differ—not being seen, being seen in the wrong way, witnessing pain, or being directly harmed.

She, too, needed care. But children share one common vulnerability: When left alone with pain they can't yet process, they almost always turn it inward. They assume they are the problem.

Maybe you carry a persistent loneliness. A nameless shame. A lingering sense of being misunderstood, unseen, or not fully known.

But what shows up most clearly in your life isn't need. What shows up instead is perfectionism, overfunctioning, withdrawal, or a compulsive tendency to please or rescue other people.

Because while the Young One holds these burdens deep inside, the Controller and the Shadow try to make up the difference in the only ways they know how—by striving for love, bracing against pain, avoiding vulnerability, or numbing what feels unbearable.

When the love you needed was absent, inconsistent, unsafe, or out of reach, a Young One inside you learned to carry burdens no child was meant to hold alone. And other parts of you learned to adapt in order to survive.

One common expression of this dynamic—one I've seen in many of my clients, and also in myself—is what psychologist Alice Miller described as *the drama of the gifted child.*[3] She wasn't referring to high IQs or special talents, but to *children who were emotionally perceptive.* These children were so attuned to the moods and needs of others that they learned to suppress their own.

In the absence of compassion and containment, these emotionally perceptive children often overcorrect. They overindex on otherwise good qualities—responsibility, peacemaking, achieving, caregiving—without learning how to tend to their own inner world.

And yet, beneath all of that strength, there is an ache you can't quite explain. A sense that something important is missing underneath.

This ache is a signature cry of the Young One.

I'm not good enough.

I'm not worth loving.

I'm on my own.

My needs don't matter.

What happened to me was my fault.

And that Young One, the one who was far too young to recognize, honor, or name her own needs, still lives in you.

And she's still sending signals, bids for connection.

When tension or stress builds, these bids can break through as moments of unexpected vulnerability: feelings that arrive all at once, seemingly out of the blue.

That's why you can suddenly feel "five years old" during a conflict with your spouse, when you're left out by a friend, or when you find yourself all alone with no one to help. It isn't regression—it's an old wound being activated in the present.

Here are some of the ways the Young One's bids may be showing up in your life:

- a sudden wave of loneliness that arrives out of nowhere, even in a crowded room
- a feeling of being small or powerless in a room full of people, even when the logical part of you knows you have every right to take up space
- an unexpected collapse into tears that feels bigger than the moment
- a flash of panic when someone pulls away or does not respond
- a secret fantasy that someone will finally notice your pain, swoop in, and give you the care you longed for

The Young One's bids often show up as a wordless ache you cannot fully explain but cannot shake. It's her way of whispering: *I'm scared. I'm alone. I need someone.*

And often, that someone is you.

Whatever burdens you carry, whatever messages you absorbed, please hear this: *These responses were never evidence of weakness.* They were evidence of *wisdom*. This was how your soul adapted when love felt uncertain or out of reach.

The work of becoming a secure soul is about meeting this Young One with compassion, curiosity, and containment—so she can finally return to Love.

FROM RESCUE TO RELATIONSHIP

In that sunlit classroom, my inner seven-year old looks so small. She's so quiet, so focused, the epitome of a tiny, burgeoning "good girl." I see the boy behind her. There *are* a lot of boys in this classroom. Her memory isn't exaggerating. (Years later, I found the class photo.)

I lean down beside her desk while she traces her spelling words.

I'm here with you, I say.

I feel my Inner Controller tugging on me to focus in on the boy behind her. *Is he okay? Is someone hurting him? Is he loved?*

Another tug points me to the playground outside the big rectangular windows, where her big sister sits alone against the brick wall with a book because the other kids won't play with her. *I don't know what to do.*

I let this part of me know that I care about her sister, and about this boy. I really do.

But right now, my attention is on this little girl, this Young One. I want to know how *she's* doing.

The classroom fades. The other children blur into the background. And suddenly it's just the two of us.

You matter too, I say gently.

And suddenly the Young One is in my arms clinging to me. I can feel her fear and the warmth of her small body, so relieved to be held.

It's okay, I whisper. *It's okay to be scared.*

I see you. I'm with you. You're not alone.

I feel her body soften, a tension releasing.

The moment feels sacred. She's lighter in my arms, secure in my presence. And then I notice something else. We're not alone. But she's already ahead of me.

She knows God is here.

Like no other part of me, this one runs straight toward God's delight, without hesitation.

She's climbing into God's arms as we are both gathered in Love. There is laughter. An ease. A safety so palpable it fills the space.

And as I watch this Young One, delighted to be with God, another insight hits me.

This is the part of me who knows how to reach for God.

The one who instinctively understands her need for God, for a Love big enough to hold her, and all the people around her.

A God strong enough to hold the scary boy and the kids who bully him.

To hold her sister.

To hold the mean girls who, even at that age, she somehow knows must have learned their meanness somewhere.

Slowly, I return my attention back to my current life, sitting here in the car where my doodles are getting groomed, across from where I went to middle school. I sense her with me still, this young girl now curled up, resting in my soul.

An inner child I'm learning to tend, with God as my faithful co-parent.

Something has shifted. The rescuing impulse has softened.

I lift my gaze. The kids I was worrying about are still there—noisy, energetic, trying to find their way. I feel genuine care for them. What an age to be so full of longing and uncertainty. I offer a prayer for them, for their teachers, for their parents.

And I stay with the truth of it: Some of these kids are held well. Some are not. That reality is hard to hold. But I can stay with the tension.

And I remember what the Young One is teaching me.

I can't rescue or save or heal everyone.

I can do my part. I can love the people in my path, in the ways I'm actually given. And I can tend to this little girl within who also needs my care.

And when the needs overwhelm, I can follow her lead.

To return to Love, again and again.

Not to bypass pain. Or minimize suffering. But to share it.

And this truth no longer feels trite. It feels real. Spacious. Strong.

Because for this Young One, God isn't an idea. God is safety. Goodness. Bigness. God *is* Love.

And I can feel more of me beginning to trust that.

My calling was never to rescue others.

It has always been to return—again and again—to the Love who can hold what I cannot.

I see now how her tenderness has shaped my desire to help others—beautifully and, at times, unhealthily. This Young One always knew of a Love big enough to heal and to save.

I just didn't know that I, too, needed that same Love.

This Young One is teaching *me*.

Because she doesn't only show us where loneliness or fear began.

She also shows us where wisdom still lives.

THE YOUNG ONE IS NOT CHILDISH—SHE IS CHILD*LIKE*.

THE WISDOM OF THE YOUNG ONE

The Young One is not childish—she is child*like*. She remembers what it means to see the world with unguarded wonder, how to trust a Love that is bigger than we are, and how to receive God's delight without hesitation.[4] Think of the children you love and their wide-eyed curiosity, their openness, the way they move through the world without yet needing to prove or protect themselves. How they want to believe that love is real. That someone bigger is good. That they are held.

It's this quality of wonder that the Young One represents.

Not naivete, but presence.

Not ignorance, but openness.

This is why Jesus' words ring so true: "Unless you change and become like little children, you will never enter the kingdom of heaven" (Matt. 18:3).

The Young One is not foolish. Nor is she cynical.

She simply knows that life is too big, and the challenges too great, to walk through it alone.

She is receptive.

And she is wise.

She gives love freely, and she takes it in.

In fact, Scripture offers a vision of this Young One as the one who will ultimately lead us. When the prophet Isaiah imagines the healing of all things, he imagines a time when creation is reconciled and violence is no more. A time when wolves lie down with lambs, lions eat straw like oxen, every wound is healed, and the natural order is remade in peace.

And at the *center* of that vision stands not a king, a warrior, or a sage—but a *child*.

"*And a little child will lead them*" (Isa. 11:6, emphasis mine).

This isn't just a poetic image or a distant hope. It's a spiritual invitation. The way forward into goodness, healing, and wholeness is not through control, performance, or self-mastery, but through the brave, uncluttered trust of a child.

THE WAY FORWARD INTO GOODNESS, HEALING, AND WHOLENESS IS NOT THROUGH CONTROL, PERFORMANCE, OR SELF-MASTERY, BUT THROUGH THE BRAVE, UNCLUTTERED TRUST OF A CHILD.

The Young One in you is not weak. She is wise.

She knows the way back to Love.

And when you finally learn to honor her voice, *everything changes*.

Sensitivity becomes strength.

Tenderness becomes courage.

Trust becomes wisdom.

Reclaimed, the Young One becomes the tender heartbeat at the center of your soul—the one who keeps choosing Love, again and again.

Recognize: *I'm wanting to rescue.*

Return: *I also need Love.*

PART THREE

HOW TO LIVE FROM A SECURE SOUL

CHAPTER 8

ANCHOR IN GOD'S LOVE

As essential as they are, your Controller, your Shadow, and the Young One do not define the whole of who you are. Each one is a precious part of your soul that is yours to reclaim and to steward. To gently notice, honor, and guide in partnership with God's Spirit.

A secure, integrated soul makes room for each of them. It honors the Controller part of you—not so that she remains the workhorse, rescuer, or perfectionist, but to honor your soul's God-made desire to show up with competence, responsibility, and perseverance. Once connected, she becomes a humble, steady guide, no longer holding your soul in a vise grip.

A secure soul also welcomes the Shadow—not so that you harbor or avoid negative emotions, but to honor your soul's capacity for pleasure, passion, and truth-telling. Once connected, she becomes a wise and honest companion. She no longer sabotages from the dark, but illuminates where comfort is needed, where beauty calls, and where integrity asks you to take a stand.

And as both learn that *you*, with God's help, are the adult in the room, they make space for the Young One to take a seat of honor at the center: the tender heart that holds longing, hope, joy, and wonder.

Over time, these scattered fragments begin to feel less like broken pieces and more like an inner sanctuary, each with its own essential role, yet far more vibrant when brought together with the others. With God as your loving co-parent, your inner soul mountain resounds with a steady melody, a soul alive with beauty, harmony, and strength.

As you learn to thank these parts for how they helped you survive, listen to the fears they still carry, and practice new, freer ways of relating, certain qualities begin to take root. These are the marks of a secure soul:

- A secure base in Love
- A sense of your worth
- The capacity to repair, even with yourself
- The freedom to risk, even when you fail
- A sense of place, even in transition
- Closeness with others, without losing yourself

This is what it means to return to Love, within yourself and with those around you, held by the One who is already here.

And the whole process is anchored within the secure base you have in Love.

WHERE THE WILD AND THE HOLY MEET

I am alone in our house. The dogs are curled up beside me, their velvet fur rising and falling with each breath. The quiet feels unfamiliar and new to this season. My husband is away for work, and our kids have both recently left—as in emptied—the nest.

Night is falling. I have a writing deadline, so I need to get down to work. The twilight hours have always been my favorite working time. But as I try to concentrate, I can't help but notice an aliveness in my bones. A sense of anticipation. Some part of me senses the excitement of being all by myself.

It's as if I'm a teenager again, home without supervision. No one to make sure I eat my vegetables. No one to tell me to turn off a show because it isn't "for girls."

Of course, no one has done those things in years. And yet, here in the silence, I feel a childlike thrill—an energy that hums just beneath the surface. The Controller in me perks up with purpose: *Use the time well. Make space for what matters most*. The Shadow chimes in, offering her own kind of wisdom: *Pour a glass of wine. Watch something that makes you laugh. Let yourself rest.*

But beneath them both, the Young One stirs. Her longing feels different. It's less about doing or unwinding and more about belonging. What she wants isn't focus or escape. It's *connection.*

My eyes drift to the window, where the mountain looms to the west in the twilight, its three peaks etched against the fading light, the same mountain I've gazed at since childhood, a steady reminder of God's presence. Below it, the trees sway in a golden stretch across the field we've never quite turned into a proper yard, reaching from our front porch straight toward the mountain.

My soul grows still, yet every part of me feels awake and attentive. The night is beckoning.

I slip out into the field in front of our small country home—out in the middle of nowhere, as they say—as darkness slowly descends. All by myself, the air holds a palpable stillness. No cars. No hum of electricity. Only the faint sound of a dog barking far off in the distance. The night feels serene yet wild, like a place that might seem dangerous if you didn't know the terrain.

And then, in that quiet expanse, something shifts. The air thickens, not with fear, but with something sacred. It's as if a Presence steps forward out of the night.

And I know, without a doubt, I am not alone.

I sense God beside me, closer than my own breath, yet wholly beyond me. It's not exactly soothing. It's so much more than that—and still, completely safe.

Peace envelops me as every detail sharpens. The moon lifts slowly into the sky, and the gentle breeze whispers across my face. In that moment, there is nowhere else I want to be. The usual swirl of worries—relationships, to-do lists, the noise of the world—evaporates.

God is here in this field, beneath this sky—filling up my soul.

No (other) miracle occurs, only the unmistakable sense of God's Presence with me.

I feel utterly secure here, under the moonlit sky, with Love itself.

Not alone.

Safe.

Held.

Even as nothing in the world around me has changed.

Later as I reflect on this moonlit walk with God, I realize that it was so much more than the fruit of "logging off" or taking a mental break. It was something transcendent, far beyond the reach of self-care or the randomness of a pleasant moment. It was intimacy. *Connectedness.*

For just a few moments, my soul caught a glimpse of what it felt like to return to the Beginning, when a human soul could walk with God in unbroken harmony.

I wasn't praying. Truthfully, I hadn't felt particularly spiritual that day. I'd been busy and distracted. And yet, in the quiet of that moment, God was already there, gently making his loving presence known to me in the golden field.

And I wonder: *Has connecting with God always been this simple?*

BEFORE BELIEF THERE WAS LOVE

Love didn't begin with belief. It began with relationship.

Long before we form ideas about God, our bodies are

learning what love feels like—whether it is safe, available, responsive, or fragile. Those early experiences settle first not in our thoughts, but in our nervous systems. And they shape how we come to experience God long before we ever have language for faith.

Trust is formed in the body long before belief takes shape in the mind.

This isn't only a psychological claim. Research suggests that human beings are born with an innate capacity for spiritual awareness—a felt sense of connection to something larger than ourselves. But like any capacity, it doesn't develop in a vacuum. It's strengthened (or constricted) by the relational world we're raised in.[1]

TRUST IS FORMED IN THE BODY LONG BEFORE BELIEF TAKES SHAPE IN THE MIND.

You first come to "know" love not through abstract ideas, but through lived experience: being held, soothed, noticed, responded to. In her book *The Birth of the Living God*, psychoanalyst Ana-Maria Rizzuto argued that just as we form inner representations of our parents—representations of love that we carry into our adult relationships—we also form an inner representation of God.[2] Over time, those embodied experiences become templates, not only for how you relate to other people, but also for how you relate to God. Your felt sense of God grows out of the same soil as your earliest attachments.

In other words, *your experience of God is shaped not only by what you* believe *about God, but also by how you first learned what love feels like.*

When love has felt steady, you tend to internalize a sense of safety. When love has felt uncertain, inconsistent, or overwhelming, you learn to brace through either working harder for closeness or shutting down. And when love is something you mostly felt through caring for others, you come to believe that the only way to feel close is to give.

YOUR EXPERIENCE OF GOD IS SHAPED NOT ONLY BY WHAT YOU *BELIEVE* ABOUT GOD, BUT ALSO BY HOW YOU FIRST LEARNED WHAT LOVE FEELS LIKE.

The problem is, most of us don't realize these patterns. We move through life carrying assumptions about love that were formed long before we chose them.

Those assumptions shape how we relate to others, how we treat ourselves, and, often most subtly, how we reach for God. When connection feels elusive, we may work to earn God's closeness. Or we may keep our distance. We might believe God is good, but if that goodness never reaches our lived experience—our emotions, our nervous system, our breath—our sense of connection might begin to fracture.

We interpret the distance as spiritual failure. Or we get angry with God. We fall back on our oldest survival strategies—strategies as ancient as the beginning of time itself. We hide in shame. Or we blame God for not showing up when we needed him most.

But what if the disconnection isn't actually about *God's presence or absence*?

What if it's *evidence of a part of your soul asking to be healed*?

WHEN GOD FEELS FAR AWAY

When I think back to that moonlit night when I sensed God's nearness, I can see now how long that moment was in the making. I've believed in God for as long as I can remember. But trust—real, embodied trust—took longer.

My mind drifts back to adolescence to a memory so vivid I can still feel the ache of it.

I'm lying in my twin bed, the yellow wallpaper of my big girl bedroom glowing faintly under the bedside lamp. My green *One Year Bible* lies open beside me, bookmarked to the exact date, next to my copy of *Graffiti: Devotions for Girls*, flipped upside down from where I have just finished reading. I've been taught to begin and end the day with God, and I do. I'm dutiful.

But what I feel on those nights isn't comfort or God's presence. It's silence, and not the healing kind of silence. Instead, what I feel is *an insurmountable brick wall between God and me.*

Night after night, I try to tear down that wall with all the spiritual fervor I can summon. I pray and plead, recite verses, and make promises to do better. I cry out to God. *But the wall will not budge.*

I blame myself. *Maybe I'm not praying enough. Maybe I'm too distracted, wanting things I shouldn't. Maybe it's wrong to want the attention of a boy, a spot on the team, a sense of being accepted. Maybe I'm not doing enough for God.*

But what I didn't know then was that the wall wasn't evidence of God's absence. Nor was it evidence of my failure.

The disconnection I felt had far less to do with me or with God—and so much more to do with *attachment*.

Though my parents were loving and supportive, like many parents in that era, they weren't emotionally attuned. As devout Christians, they established strict rules to keep us safe. *Don't drink. Don't date boys. Don't stay out after 10 p.m. Don't go to R-rated movies. Forget about parties.* My older sister and I would watch *Footloose* over and over in those days, identifying with Lori Singer's frustration with her loving but harsh disciplinarian father. We just wanted to *dance* every once in a while—or at least see an R-rated movie.

And somehow, in the absence of emotional attunement—even in a loving family—a part of me picked up the idea that goodness was what earned connection, and that the shadowy part of me who longed for love was the problem. I internalized the image of a distant, carrot-holding God—loving, yes, but just out of reach.

Without a model for emotional intimacy, I learned to associate *closeness* with attuning to others through caring, noticing, and tending. I conflated closeness with empathy, experiencing nearness when I entered into someone else's pain. While that capacity became a gift in my life, it also distorted how I experienced connection with others and with God, especially in those formative years.

I was reaching for God in the only way I knew—through effort. Through performance. Through doing what I thought God needed. And yet, I felt anything but connected.

It took me years to see what was really happening beneath the surface: The problem wasn't that God was absent; it was that the circuitry for the kind of intimacy I longed for hadn't yet been formed.

NEURAL PATHWAYS

What I experienced as a wall between God and me wasn't God's absence. It was the limit of what my nervous system knew how to receive.

As psychiatrist Curt Thompson writes in *Anatomy of the Soul*, the brain's capacity for emotional intimacy develops through *lived experiences of safety and responsiveness.*[3] Over time, those experiences carve neural pathways in the brain, internalized patterns that help the nervous system recognize what love feels like and whether it's safe to take in. Those patterns don't only impact how we experience other people. They also have spiritual implications. The same neural pathways that allow us to register human love are involved in how we perceive divine love.

This helps explain something many people carry: You can believe in God with your mind while parts of your soul struggle to register that belief as comfort, safety, or closeness. That gap isn't necessarily rebellion or spiritual failure. More often, it's a painful mismatch between longing and capacity.

Capacity isn't about how sincere you are. It isn't about how many verses you've read, or how hard you've tried to pray. Capacity is the *felt* ability to let love in without bracing. It's what happens in your body when closeness comes near:

Do you soften? Do you open enough to let warmth in?

Or do you tighten? Do you scramble or work harder, trying to secure what you fear might disappear?

Do you stay present? Or do you brace and deflect?

The answers to these questions often have less to do with what's happening in the present moment and more to do with what your nervous system learned long ago about closeness and safety.

You might think of it like a receiver. Love can be present and real, but if the inner circuitry hasn't been shaped to receive it, the signal doesn't register as comfort.

In my case, God's love was present, but it registered to my system as a brick wall. That's often what it feels like when longing outpaces what the nervous system has been taught to hold.

This is why attachment is so important. It's not about blaming the past; it's about understanding what your body learned to expect from love . . . and what it can still learn.

Because here is the good news: *Your capacity to experience safety and receive love can grow.* It's one reason the experience of a first love—or a deep, steady friendship—can feel almost spiritual. Something in you softens. New pathways of trust begin to form. Love is encountered in a new way. It can feel like a rebirth, not because that person is divine, but because a safe relationship becomes a living context where old attachment wounds begin to loosen.

And this is true spiritually too. Just as you can learn to trust other people in deeper and more meaningful ways, you can also learn slowly and gently to trust God in every part of your soul, not only in your beliefs.

Often, it starts simply: by recognizing your own attachment patterns.

ATTACHMENT AND GOD

Decades of research suggest that the way we first learned to give and receive love often echoes in how we reach for the Divine.[4]

A part of you may worry about disappointing God or being abandoned by him. You might pray often or serve tirelessly, hoping to stay close to God's favor. This neglected, often long-overlooked part of you longs for the reassurance that you are still loved.

None of these practices are the problem. Prayer, service, and devotion are beautiful expressions of love. The problem is when they become a way to earn love—when you relate to God the way a child tries to secure a parent's affection by being good, responsible, or pleasing. Inevitably, another part of you grows tired—exhausted, unseen, or burnt out.

Or, a part of you might think it's too risky to depend on God. You may keep God at arm's length. This tough-on-the-surface part of you leans on self-sufficiency, certainty, or willpower.

Again, it's not wrong to be independent, thoughtful, or even highly disciplined. The problem is when independence becomes a way to avoid intimacy. A part of you learns to relate to God the way a child tries to stay safe by needing less, feeling less, and asking for nothing. Inevitably, another part of you feels distant, cut off, or lonely.

Of course our attachment wounds aren't the only reason God can feel far away. Sometimes we do have the capacity, and yet we resist God through pride, conscious self-protection, or sin. And even then love breaks through anyway, often in flashes of grace we can't explain. Still, attachment is often at work underneath the surface, especially when there's an ache in your soul that doesn't seem to resolve despite all your best efforts.

Whether you move anxiously toward God and work hard to earn closeness, or pull avoidantly away from God and stay wary of vulnerability or need, both are ultimately about trust. And the underlying longing is the same. *Your soul longs for closeness that feels safe*. What differs isn't the longing, but the strategies that formed around it.

Your Controller may strive, perform, or tighten into certainty and control. And your Inner Shadow may pull back, resist, or harden into quiet resentment or cynicism. These strategies aren't failures of faith. They are bids for connection, reminders that some part of your soul is still in need.

The problem is that in many faith communities, we subtly reward the Controller and misunderstand the Shadow. We praise tireless spiritual effort, but we tend to correct or distrust anger, disappointment, and distance.

But the truth is: *neither extreme* reflects secure attachment. Both postures grow out of pain. Both protect us from the risk of real intimacy—with others, and with God.

So what's the solution?

As theologian N. T. Wright reminds us, the story of Scripture isn't about escaping this world for heaven, but about *heaven coming here*. God's presence has already entered into this world and is already restoring creation from the inside out.[5] Applied to the parts of your soul, this means healing doesn't wait for some far-off day when we leave this earth. God enters into these very places now—not to remove the ache of vulnerability, but to gently meet us in it.

From an attachment perspective, Wright's reminder is profound. God meets your Controller right here—not shaming its effort, but slowly teaching this part of you that love does not have to be earned. God also meets your Shadow—not condemning its hesitance, but showing this part of you that closeness does not have to overwhelm. As your Controller learns to trust and your Shadow learns to soften, the Young One is freed to do what she was always meant to do: receive Love precisely where your soul is most tender.

GOD IS NOT OUR ESCAPE HATCH FROM HUMAN VULNERABILITY. GOD IS OUR ANCHOR *WITHIN IT*.

God is not our escape hatch from human vulnerability. God is our anchor *within it*.

Your attachment patterns don't have to define your future. Divine Love doesn't ask you to bypass the ways you've learned to survive *but to recognize them*—and return, again and again, to Love.

Which means healing isn't about trying harder to believe. Healing is about *trying softer*, as my friend and fellow therapist Aundi Kolber said so beautifully.[6] It's about slowly expanding your capacity to receive love.

RECEIVING LOVE

That's what I began to understand years later when I returned to the fourteen-year-old girl lying awake in her yellow bedroom, trying to tear down the wall she felt between herself and God.

I don't approach her with judgment. I come with love.

I recognize the relentlessness of her Inner Controller—not as arrogance or spiritual pride, but as devotion shaped by longing: *Pray harder. Mean it more. Stay awake until you feel something.* She believes closeness is earned through effort, because that's how connection has always worked for her. And yet, no matter how many verses she reads or how long she stays awake, the wall stays put.

I also recognize the Shadow's voice—sharp, scolding, cruel. *If you really loved God, you'd feel him.* Her words cut deep, and for years a part of me believes them. Believes that the silence on the other side of that wall must be my fault.

But beneath both of those voices is something far more tender.

I can sense the longing of the Young One: *I ache to be held, to feel seen, to know someone is here with me.*

I am filled with compassion for her. What a beautiful longing. And what a painful thing to feel so alone.

In my mind I can see ahead of her. I think about how in a few years, she will discover the love of a kind boy, a love that finds its way past her walls. And then a dear friend, a true kindred spirit. A mentor, several teachers, and Stacy, her therapist colleague who will one day come and scoop her up when she is most in need. And one day, she will find the steady, lasting love of a really good man, one who sees her fully, both the intensity of her Inner Controller and the shame of her swearing Inner Shadow, and stays.

Each of these relationships will carry a thread of this love—God's love—she was aching to find. Each one God's way of whispering, "*This is what love feels like.*" Each relationship will become a stitch, slowly mending what was torn, teaching her that love can be safe. Intimate. Fully received.

I hold these stories on her behalf. And then I gently turn toward her.

I want her to know I am with her in *this* moment.

I know you feel so alone right now, I tell her softly. *But please know you won't always feel this way. This wall is not your fault. It's not a failure of faith. It's the growing pains of your soul reaching toward something you haven't yet been shown how to receive.*

LONGING IS NOT THE ABSENCE OF LOVE. IT IS LOVE ARRIVING BEFORE IT CAN BE HELD.

You have such a beautiful capacity for love. And right now, your longing is larger than your ability to hold what you long for. That doesn't mean something is wrong with you. It means your soul is wise.

This ache isn't failure. It's a sign that your soul is still learning it's safe to receive. And when love does come, it will mean all the more because you have longed so deeply.

She softens, still unsure, but open. *So there's nothing wrong with me?*

No, sweet one. Not at all.

I bless her longing for connection. I bless her ache. I hate that she feels it so sharply. And yet I see now that it's the mark of a soul reaching for what is good, for what is real, for what she was always meant to receive.

I didn't know this then, but the wall was never proof that I had failed God. It was a signal that my soul didn't yet know how to recognize the love it was made to receive.

The ache wasn't a failure, it was pointing somewhere *true.*

Longing is not the absence of love. It is love arriving before it can be held.

I want her to know that this yearning, this ache, is not in vain.

That, in the words of John Mayer, "*Good love is on the way*,"[7] or as another songwriter, Solomon, wrote, "He has made everything beautiful in its time" (Eccl. 3:11).

And I want the same for you.

RETURN TO LOVE

Have you ever ached to feel God's love but couldn't seem to find it?

Or maybe you once felt God's nearness, but over time, it faded.

What if the distance you feel with God was never proof of your weakness?

What if it was never a failure of faith, but a signal that part of your soul never received the love it needed? Or worse, received harm instead of love?

Other parts of you have been trying so valiantly to help

in the only ways they knew how. They believe if you tried harder, prayed longer, stayed in control—or if you numbed out, pulled away, or even lashed out at God—you might somehow earn love, or at least manage the ache of not having it.

But what if the answer was never more effort? Never more shame?

What if the answer has always been Love?

Every time you return to a hurting part of yourself with compassion, you're strengthening new pathways for closeness.

Every time you risk receiving the love of another person—someone who sees you and stays—your nervous system learns that closeness can be safe.

Over time, those new pathways grow stronger than the old ones. *What once felt like a wall of disconnection becomes a bridge of trust.*

Wherever you find yourself, know this: God *is* the Loving Presence who does not leave.

In the beginning, God didn't love from afar; he *walked with* humanity "in the cool of the day" (Gen. 3:8). Love was known as a *presence*, felt in the body, sensed in nearness, woven through breath and attention.

As the apostle John wrote, "*God is love*" (1 John 4:8, emphasis added). And good love—God's love—is *always* on the way.

That night, when I walked out under the moonlit sky and sensed God's presence, it wasn't that God hadn't been there on the other days. It was that, through the slow work of becoming a secure soul, *every part of me was finally learning what it feels like to trust the fullness of Love.*

The simple beauty of that moment didn't come with age, or effort, or even decades of going to church. It came through returning to the places inside me that hadn't yet known love—and gently introducing them to it.

Over time, as I've learned to recognize and tend to the parts of my soul, I've discovered what that fourteen-year-old girl was so desperate to find—a deep, abiding intimacy with God. Not dramatic answers to desperate pleas, at least not often. Not flashy miracles. But something even more profound and far more sustaining: steady, faithful moments of loving Presence.

ONE DAY, YOU'LL SEE IT CLEARLY: YOU WERE NEVER CHASING LOVE ALL THOSE YEARS. LOVE WAS *ALWAYS* CHASING YOU.

Every part of your soul is slowly being rewired for Love.

And the very places in you that ache the most become the soil most fertile to receive it.

This work of tending to these places within isn't abstract.

It isn't peripheral.

It's the sacred work of returning—again and again—to Love.

And one day, you'll see it clearly: You were never chasing love all those years.

Love was *always* chasing you.

No fracture is too insignificant. No ache too small.

Every act of return, every moment of connection, reminds us that we are still held by the same Love who first walked with us in the beginning.

Recognize: *I'm aching for God.*

Return: *I am loved, even here.*

CHAPTER 9

KNOW YOU WERE WORTH LOVING ALL ALONG

What we often call *worth* might be better named *belovedness.* Because worth is initially felt (or not felt) in relationship.

A secure soul isn't one that never doubts its worth. It's one that keeps returning to belovedness.

When we talk about worth as something rooted in the self, it can start to sound like a possession, like something to claim, defend, or prove. But true worth isn't self-generated. It's *bestowed.* It's the quiet dignity that flows from being made by Love, for Love.

From a spiritual lens, your worth simply *is.* The objective reality of your worth is constant, like gravity, holding you even when you can't feel it. But psychologically, your capacity to *feel* that worth can very much come and go.

A SECURE SOUL ISN'T ONE THAT NEVER DOUBTS ITS WORTH. IT'S ONE THAT KEEPS RETURNING TO BELOVEDNESS.

I know this pattern well.

WHEN WORTH FEELS LIKE A COMPETITION

I'm sitting in my living room, pretending to scroll through emails, but my mind is somewhere else entirely. It's trapped in a social media post I saw earlier this morning.

My colleague didn't get the gig.

The thing I thought she would. The thing I feared she would.

And I'm not proud of this, but a flicker of relief moves through me. A flicker that feels . . . good.

It's not spiteful or mean-spirited. Just a subtle exhale, a moment of reprieve from the ache of comparison.

It's the absence of what I didn't want to feel: the emotional backlash, the avalanche of shame and not-enoughness that can sometimes follow someone else's win.

Maybe you've felt it too—that secret sense of ease when someone else doesn't succeed. It's not that you want them to fail. It's just that their success can sometimes feel like a mirror, reflecting your doubts about your own *worth*.

I don't even know this woman well. She's not unkind. But she hasn't really ever given me the time of day. And it hurts. And when she shines, I feel like I disappear.

A shadowy part of me doesn't want her to fail exactly; it just doesn't want her to win.

And that part startles me.

It doesn't fit with how I want to see myself.

But what I've learned is this: That first flicker of relief isn't cruelty; it's *fear.*

Fear that there's only so much spotlight to go around.

Fear that if someone else shines, there won't be any light left for her.

Fear that someone else's triumph is in some way a reflection on her own *worth.*

I close my eyes and put my hand on my heart. And I ask the question I've learned to ask when the shadowy emotions emerge:

What do you need, my love?

And instantly, I feel her warmth inside of me. She responds to my presence.

THE GATEKEEPERS OF YOUR WORTH

You may have your own version of this story.

Maybe it shows up when you're scrolling late at night and your stomach tightens at someone else's announcement, or a photo of their family that looks far more perfect than your own.

Maybe it appears when a friend doesn't get the thing she hoped for, and you feel a quiet, unspoken relief.

Without even realizing it, your mind might drift toward comparisons you make with other people—how often they're invited, how easily their work seems to be recognized or rewarded, how put-together their lives appear, or the ease money seems to bring.

And you might notice the shadowy emotions that rise up almost imperceptibly: envy, self-doubt, that familiar sense of less-than. Somewhere deep within lives a part of you that still remembers being left out, overlooked, or unseen.

A SENSE OF WORTH ISN'T ARGUED INTO EXISTENCE. IT'S FORMED THROUGH *RELATIONSHIP*—THROUGH BEING SEEN, VALUED, AND HELD OVER TIME.

That part of you isn't trying to sabotage you; she's giving you a *bid for connection*. She's struggling to remember the truth that you are beloved, even here.

You can tell yourself that you should know better, that you shouldn't feel this way.

But some part of you isn't buying it.

A sense of worth isn't argued into existence. It's formed through *relationship*—through being seen, valued, and held over time.

Remember, your experience of love didn't begin with belief. It began with relationship. The same is true for worth.

Think of a young child scanning for safety. In healthy environments, she looks up and finds a steady, attuned presence—a parent, teacher, or caregiver who mirrors back her dignity: *You are seen. You matter. You're beloved.*

Someone who stays with her and helps her find her way. Over time, that sense of dignity, of worth, becomes internalized.

But when attunement is absent, inconsistent, or conditional—when there's no one to help you carry the uncertainty about your worth—you start carrying it alone. And that's when parts of you rise up to protect you from the ache of doubting your own dignity, your own inherent value, your own *self.*

The Controller tightens her grip, believing that if you just work harder, achieve more, perfect better, or outshine others, you can finally secure your value. Comparison becomes fuel for striving.

And when all that striving still fails to earn the deep, settled sense of worth you crave, the Shadow steps in. She tries to *dull the sting* of feeling unseen, unnoticed, or not enough through numbing, self-shaming, resentment, or by quietly rooting against others' success. She builds a shield against the ache.

As you now know, these parts of you aren't trying to sabotage you. They're stepping in to help where a secure sense of worth has not fully taken root.

Your Inner Controller doesn't yet realize that worth can't be earned by proving yourself in the eyes of others, and that all of her efforts only keep you on a never-ending hamster wheel.

Your Inner Shadow doesn't yet realize that shaming yourself or resenting others only keeps you orbiting the ever-moving target of other people's approval and recognition.

The truth is that both of these parts are gatekeepers.

They are the *keepers of your longing.* Each one holds vigil over the Young One within, who still remembers, and aches for, a sense of her belovedness.

THE WOUND OF WORTH

As I gently recognize the shadowy part of me—the one feeling relief at my colleague's lack of success—the answer to my query, *What is it you need, my love?* comes quickly.

I want to be chosen.

I want to be seen.

I don't want to disappear again.

This isn't malice. It's *longing.*

Old longing.

The kind that forms around kitchen tables and closed bedroom doors, at middle school cafeterias, team tryouts, and school dances.

I breathe with her. I stay.

She's not more than fourteen. She doesn't need to be banished. She needs to be *understood.*

My mind flashes to eighth-grade basketball tryouts, to that moment when I did everything right and *still* didn't make the team. I beat her. I *beat* the other tiny, toothpick-legged girl in our one-on-one matchup. And it didn't matter. I still wasn't chosen. And she *was.*

There was only room for one of us.

She was in. I was out.

I can still feel my heart sink as my eyes traveled down the

list of girls who made the team, posted in our locker room. My name wasn't on the list. Not on varsity. Not on JV. Not on any list at all.

Shame rushed in. I had worked so hard, practicing every day after school. Free throws. Layups. Dribbling. *Why did I even bother?*

I swallowed my pride and became the team manager. I sat on the sidelines, behind a large desk, taking stats and filling water bottles, while the other girls ran up and down the court, sharpened skills, and learned how to form a *team* together. They *belonged* with each other.

My Inner Controller buried her head in those stats. She told me to double down on the work of helping the coach and supporting the team.

The Shadow part of me told me it was my fault. I just wasn't as good as the other girls.

One day, some girls were out sick, and the coach called over to me, "Hey Alison, suit up. We need you to practice with us today."

I couldn't believe it. I raced to the locker room, pulled on my gym clothes, and ran onto the court. For a fleeting moment, I was one of the girls. *I was on the team.*

During practice, one of the team captains turned to me and said, "Hey, Toothpick—you're pretty good!" I didn't mind when *she* called me toothpick. I beamed. I felt proud. I *belonged*. At least for that moment.

For two days, I practiced with the team. I passed. I shot. I sweat. I laughed. I stayed late. My heart soared as I secretly fantasized about the coach recognizing his mistake. Surely he'd see my talent. Surely he'd open up a spot on the team for me.

Then the other girls came back.

Still, I showed up, dressed and ready to play. But the coach looked at me and said, "We don't need you anymore, kid. Thanks for stepping in."

That was it.

I was back on the sidelines.

Back behind my plywood desk.

Back to that profound feeling of not being *chosen.*

I don't belong.

I'm not good enough.

My worth is up for debate.

I turn back to my morning scroll in my current adult life, to the moment when I noticed a quiet, unsettling relief that someone else hadn't succeeded. I shake my head.

This part of me runs deep—the one who can feel as if she's still sitting on the sidelines, unsure if she fully belongs, wondering if her worth will always be up for debate.

This is the ache the Shadow has been guarding all along.

THE TRANSFORMATION OF THE SHADOW

My guess is you might have moments like these too—times when not being chosen slowly rearranges how you experience your own value.

This is the wound of worth.

It forms when connection feels scarce, when love feels conditional, when being chosen seems reserved for someone else. And when this wound goes unacknowledged, the

Shadow steps in. She's not trying to destroy you; she's trying to protect you from disappearing altogether.

You tell yourself you should be able to shrug it off. That you shouldn't care what others think. That you should be stronger, thicker-skinned, more grateful, more mature—*better* somehow.

But those *shoulds* don't heal. They're the voice of your Inner Controller trying, once again, to secure your worth through effort, correction, or control, through valiantly trying to manage what only Love can hold in your inner world. It doesn't work.

WHEN YOU STOP FIGHTING YOUR INNER EXPERIENCE, YOU CAN BEGIN TO SHAPE IT.

What does work is far gentler and far braver.

It begins when you *meet yourself* right there *in* the shadowy places.

When you begin to notice the feelings you'd rather not admit—resentment, shame, envy, self-criticism, that less-than feeling—not with condemnation but with presence.

You don't meet yourself there to stay there. You meet yourself to name what's true.

I see that you're comparing yourself.

I get that you feel less-than.

I can sense the resentment stirring.

Naming doesn't encourage the feelings. It softens them. It's a kind of confession, a powerful way to bring what's been hidden into the safety of relationship.

I'm here.

I'm not afraid of these feelings.

I'll stay as long as it takes.

And something begins to shift.

When you stop fighting your inner experience, you can begin to shape it.

Here's what I have seen again and again, in my own life and in the lives of so many others: This part of you that carries these shadowy emotions doesn't have to be your downfall.

She can become a doorway.

As you work with the whole truth—the shadowy feelings and the wound beneath them—clarity emerges. And clarity gives birth to freedom.[1]

Naming what's hard is telling the truth. It's the restoration of dignity.

Naming restores agency. Agency restores a sense of worth.

This is hard.

I wish I didn't feel this way.

But I do.

All of this can be true.

And from that place of safety, something steadier grows. You give yourself the gift of honesty. The gift of compassion. The gift of being seen, held, and known, even in the shadowy places.

NAMING RESTORES AGENCY. AGENCY RESTORES A SENSE OF WORTH.

Here's what is true: God doesn't drive the Shadow deeper into hiding.

Love holds out a hand.

Love doesn't demand that the Shadow become shiny. Love invites her to become honest. And when her honesty is received with tenderness, secrecy loses its grip.

What was once a place of hiding becomes a place of freedom.

And when this shadowy part of your soul dares to trust Love, dares to tell the truth about herself and what she feels, something remarkable happens.

She becomes the *Seer* within you.

The Shadow's deepest gift has *always* been her refusal to pretend. The damage was never in the dark feelings themselves. It came from *disconnecting from Love* in order to deny them—or act out of them.

When you meet her with compassion and containment, she slowly begins to transform. Raw emotion becomes discernment. Intensity becomes insight. Suspicion becomes wisdom.

This kind of change doesn't come through force. It comes through *presence*.

When the Shadow feels the safe, steady containment of being *seen*, instead of shamed or punished, something deeper begins to surface. The Shadow no longer has to fight for your worth. She becomes brave enough to help you tell a different story.

THE STORY OF YOUR WORTH

As I reflect on the different parts of my soul, the different parts of my story, I can see so much more clearly how it all began to shape my sense of worth.

Not just the dutiful middle-school girl on the sidelines of that basketball court, but the many moments, all threaded together, stretching back to the root.

The focused young girl, buried in her algebra books.

The shadowy one, swearing into her journal.

The earnest one, crying out to God and meeting a brick wall.

And the even younger one, always watching others, learning to read the room, becoming attentive to what was needed, never quite realizing that she, too, needed love.

Each of these moments, small and ordinary in their own way, wove together a larger story about my worth, shaped by the same essential questions:

Do I matter?

Am I worth loving?

I'm guessing you have your own string of moments—your own memories—each one quietly telling a story of your worth.

And you can learn to meet yourself in those places, exactly where those questions first took root. You can learn to tell a different story as God's presence reveals the truth of your belovedness: *Your worth has never been up for debate. Not now. Not ever.*

This is where healing begins: not in erasing the past, but in returning again and again to the truth of your belovedness.

The ache doesn't always vanish right away, but when it's met, when your soul is held within the steady gaze of Love, you slowly learn to trust.

Comparison gives way to compassion.

Proving gives way to presence.

Striving gives way to steadiness.

You can honor the worth of others because their worth is no longer a threat to yours.

When you listen to the story of your soul with compassion, when you bring each moment, each part of you, into the presence of Love, something sacred unfolds.

Your soul learns that your worth was never earned by performance nor revoked by rejection.

Your soul is and always has been *Beloved.*

Because beneath every harsh word, every jealous impulse, every quiet withdrawal lies one sacred question:

Am I loved, even here?

And the answer is yes. Always, yes.

Recognize: *I feel unworthy.*

Return: *I am loved, even here.*

CHAPTER 10

BRAVE THE PATH TO (INNER) REPAIR

We often think of repair as something that happens *between* people, in that moment after a conflict when healing words are exchanged, apologies are made, and trust is slowly rebuilt. But rupture and repair also happen *within* you and with God.

Every soul knows the ache of inner rupture. Sometimes it's the anger or disappointment you feel toward yourself. Other times it's the pain of feeling that someone else broke something in you—and you don't know how to mend it.

A secure soul isn't one that never rips. It's one that's learned how to tend to the tear.

Whether that tending unfolds in a relationship or within your inner world, the movement of repair is the same: It's the courage to face what was hurt, the persistence to stay when it's hard, and the humility to let Love in—again and again.

A SECURE SOUL ISN'T ONE THAT NEVER RIPS. IT'S ONE THAT'S LEARNED HOW TO TEND TO THE TEAR.

Repair is the sacred art of turning toward what feels broken inside, of placing a gentle touch on a bruised place in your soul and tending it until it begins to heal. It's the slow, courageous work of noticing disconnection and inviting God into that very place. And often it includes forgiveness, even for yourself.

MEETING REGRET

I'm thirty-seven—years before the life I have now—dating the man who will become my husband. He's a widower with two young children, and I've fallen in love with all three of them.

So I'm surprised by what happens when I learn that their babysitter, more of a family member, really, is pregnant. She's twenty-seven, happily married, glowing, on the cusp of a new chapter.

This young woman came into their lives several years prior, when my husband's first wife was diagnosed with a terminal illness. Over that brutal year, and through her death, this young woman helped carry the family—picking the kids up from school and helping hold everything together.

When I entered the picture, she gently bridged the tender transition from the children's attachment to her steady presence to their slowly growing attachment to me. She is truly an angel, a gift in all our lives, and she has also become a friend.

And yet, every time I see her growing belly, a wave of grief washes over me.

It isn't envy. I know that feeling, and this is something different. It's *grief*—waves of sadness I haven't known before.

I can't explain it at first. Most of me is overflowing with gratitude for this new life God has given me and for this family he is gently knitting together. But a part of me hears the haunting whisper of *if only.*

If only I'd figured out how to find someone earlier. Maybe I, too, might have been pregnant at twenty-seven, or thirty, or thirty-two, like so many of my friends. *If only* I'd known then how to let someone in. *If only* I hadn't missed my window.

I'll soon learn that I am indeed past my window for having a baby biologically, a possibility some part of me had sensed.

But I also feel a vague sense of remorse. And the remorse surprises me.

So I turn to this remorseful part of me that has suddenly surfaced. I don't try to talk her out of her feelings. Instead, I ask God to help me meet her in them.

I see her in a flannel shirt, ponytail pulled tight. No longer a toothpick. This younger version of me is twenty-seven, several years before the panic attacks that would leave her sleeping in her colleague's son's bedroom. She's hunched over a stack of books in a large university research library beneath fluorescent lights, complete with long tables, threadbare orange carpet, and shelves built for studies and journals, not comfort. Curled up so far into her mind that she's hardly aware of the shadowy loneliness all around her.

I can feel her intensity as she pores over every word, underlining the quotes she loves most. Wrestling with psychology. Finding refuge in theology. Trying to braid big ideas into something that makes sense. Alone, and almost entirely lost in her own mind.

I feel compassion for her, in addition to respect. I'm not here to judge her. I'm here to connect.

Something in her softens, here in my presence.

It's as though she senses the grief I'm carrying. She's beginning to wonder with me about what it means.

You mean, I *kept us from . . . having a baby?* she volunteers cautiously.

I think of how divided I was—retreating into work, disappearing into fantasy, and keeping so much of myself walled off that real intimacy was impossible. My Controller was trying to keep me safe, but in the process she kept the whole system locked down, still shaped by the old fear that longing itself was the problem.

Maybe, I say gently. *I don't know. I do know that some of our strategies weren't very helpful in finding the kind of love that grows a family.*

I don't want to shame her. She wasn't making these choices in a vacuum. There were real obstacles and pressures at work around her.

And the truth is I *don't* know. I may not have met someone, even if I'd known how to take down my walls earlier. Many wonderful women don't. But I also don't want to offer her something that isn't sincere. Because the truth is, I did play a part in my own delayed journey to love and family.

I also don't rush to add, *But God redeemed our story*, even though that is equally true. For now, I am curious about her growing awareness of the role she has played in my current life.

So I simply stay with her.

I didn't know, she whispers.

I know you didn't, my adult self responds.

I thought I was helping by staying focused on studies, by trying to never be a bother. I thought I could keep all that pain away. I didn't know how to do it any differently.

I know, I say again. Not to shame her, but to honor the sincerity of her reflection.

I'm sorry, she whispers.

My eyes fill with tears as I stay with her.

It's okay, my dear one. I love who you were. And I love who we're still becoming.

And I sense God's love with us as we share this moment, knitting us together and mending the space between the younger version of me once trapped in her mind, and the adult I'm still becoming.

THE GRACE OF HONEST SEEING

What happened here is the grace of honest seeing, the moment when a younger self within is met with enough safety to face a truth it couldn't yet hold. Often, it's only in adulthood, with compassion and support, that we can look back and recognize how earlier versions of us were shaping our choices.

Here's the truth about attachment wounds: The disconnected parts of your soul mountain don't disappear just because you reach adulthood. They linger, shaping how you love, how you protect yourself, and the paths you choose.

Sometimes those younger parts of you can draw you into patterns that cause real pain in your adult life. Not because you're broken or naive, but because those parts of you are still doing the best they know how to do. For example, maybe some part of you lured you into:

- Entering a relationship that wasn't safe
- Staying too long in a job you hated
- Numbing with food, alcohol, relationships, or anything to quiet the ache
- Driving yourself past exhaustion, relentlessly chasing a sense of "enough"
- Resisting therapy or ignoring medical care
- Attempting to "rescue" someone else, only to lose yourself in the process

Sometimes the cost is high. Sometimes it's mildly frustrating. I still regret the part of me that never cultivated the discipline of exercising. It's harder to develop when you're fifty!

THE SECURE SOUL LEARNS THAT IT DOESN'T HELP TO BLAME YOUR YOUNGER SELF FOR WHAT SHE DIDN'T KNOW.

Regardless of what part of your story you look back on with a twinge of heartache, grief, or regret, you can still repair the rupture. The secure soul learns that it doesn't help to blame your younger self for what she didn't know. Nor does it help to harbor resentment, regret, or inner frustration.

True repair isn't about laying blame or trying to tuck away flickering feelings of shame, frustration, or regret. It's the courage to look at your own choices, your own patterns, and say, *Yes, I see how that part of me shaped my story. I can repair that inner fracture. And I can heal and grow so that old patterns aren't repeated.*

Of course, there may be real blame to name. Maybe you let yourself down through a poor choice, or an ongoing pattern of choices. Maybe you were let down by others—if you'd been guided differently, protected more fully, seen or loved better, you might not have had to learn the hard way. Maybe if someone hadn't exploited your good faith, you'd be in a different place today.

Naming those realities matters. That's part of truth-telling too.

Naming is where we begin. But repair is how we actually heal and move forward.

And the truth is: You can't always repair with another person. But you can always repair with yourself. And the work we're doing here—the work of *inner repair*—is ultimately about what happens within you.

Repair is the work of honoring the truth of what happened without slipping into blame or self-condemnation. It allows you to name what was real while also recognizing that you made the best decisions you could with the knowledge, support, and capacity you had at the time.

And God's presence makes this process even more possible, even more secure. Divine Love provides a safe container where we can hold regret, remorse, and grief without collapsing into it.

Repair doesn't erase the past, but it does loosen its grip over you—freeing you to heal more deeply and move forward with greater wisdom.

That's the tender miracle of repair: learning to mend the torn places within your soul while staying rooted in Love.

It starts with paying attention to your soul's bids for connection.

MEETING YOUR PAST SELF

Here's the paradox: Your soul's bid to repair often surfaces when you have finally found your way to a better place. It often emerges once you've found some safety, a sense of solid ground. You settle into a healthier relationship, a more life-giving work environment, or a nourishing community. And then, almost out of nowhere, you begin to hear the voice of *if only:*

If only I'd left that toxic relationship sooner, I would have saved so much time.

If only I hadn't left that relationship—I regret the pain I caused.

If only I had fought for my dreams—I wasted so many years.

If only I had been a more attentive parent/spouse/friend, I might not feel this regret.

This voice is the bid of a younger part of you reaching out for connection. And here's the good news: These younger parts of your soul tend to surface only *when there's finally enough safety to be seen.* They wait beneath the surface of your life, watching to see if the ground will hold. When stability begins to take root—when love proves a little more consistent, when peace lasts a little longer than the chaos once did—these tender places within you start to stir.

It's as if they whisper, *Is it safe now? Can I come out? Will you stay with me if I do?*

It can feel uncomfortable, initially, to face these parts of you. They call to mind painful seasons, unearthing moments, decisions, and patterns you'd rather not revisit. Over time, parts of you may have grown adept at pushing those pain points away. You learn to minimize. Justify. Or hold regret.

But the echoes remain:

Why did I let that happen?

Why didn't anyone help me?

Why didn't I know better?

These younger parts of your soul need your attention and care. And they need to be reconnected to Love. They need to be gently updated on what you know now that you couldn't have known then. They need to learn—not with head knowledge, but through your presence—that there is more safety, connection, and love here than they once thought possible. And sometimes they need to know that you forgive them.

It is so freeing and so powerful when you can sit beside even the most painful moments of your story and whisper to a younger version of yourself:

I understand why you made that choice.

I see how hard you were working to keep me safe.

I'm here with you now. I'm not leaving.

I forgive you.

I love you.

You are welcome here with me.

You don't look back to relive the past, to blame or shame yourself, or to linger in regret. You look back to *reclaim the part of you who's still stuck there* and to guide her into the present. In doing so, you not only experience more wholeness, but you also identify and transform patterns, echoes of which still linger.

REPAIRING WITH YOURSELF

When I reconnected with that twenty-seven-year-old version of me—the one living in her mind as a protective form of self-sufficiency—I saw patterns that *can and do* still surface. I don't wish to shame that part of me. But I do wish to remind myself to *stay alert*. Old patterns can resurface.

When you turn toward a younger version of yourself with compassion and really seek to understand that place where injury occurred, you invite real healing, and the opportunity for growth, into the very place where the wound still lives. That shift from contempt to compassion opens the door to greater trust and deeper integration.

Decades of research on self-compassion echo what lived experience already tells us: Meeting yourself with kindness doesn't make you complacent. It makes you more honest, more accountable, and more capable of meaningful change.[1]

And often, it leads to self-forgiveness.

You might think of this as the paradox of forgiveness—a paradox that applies both to forgiving others and to forgiving parts of yourself. Practicing genuine self-forgiveness doesn't mean excusing the past or minimizing pain or regret. Instead, it means telling the truth about what happened, taking responsibility for what's yours to own, and extending compassion to yourself as you choose new ways forward.

REAL FORGIVENESS IS HOLDING BOTH ACCOUNTABILITY AND COMPASSION AT THE SAME TIME.

Real forgiveness is holding both accountability and compassion at the same time.

Studies have found that this kind of deep-down self-forgiveness reduces shame, strengthens emotional health, and builds resilience.[2] When you gently uncover a wounded place within your soul, a place where you're harboring guilt, shame, or regret, you can:

1. Identify the patterns and choices that didn't serve you well.
2. Take responsibility for what you didn't know then but do know now.
3. Grieve and grow, as you honor what was lost, and take steps to live differently today.

This is what happened in my own story. The paradox of safety is that the very love and security I found when I met my now-husband awakened a place within I had buried.

From the safety of this new love, I began to look back and reexamine choices I had made years earlier.

I had already learned the hard way that avoiding painful emotions never works. So when that voice of *if only* rose within me, I didn't push it away. I paid attention to it. And that work only strengthened the bonds I share with my now-family. In fact, our ability to hold love and grief together—to speak of both and to share them with one another—is what draws us into deeper intimacy. It's what has made us as strong, perhaps even stronger in some ways, as many families bound only by blood.

WHEN YOU ALLOW YOURSELF TO HOLD BOTH LOVE AND SORROW TOGETHER, YOU MAKE SPACE FOR A DEEPER KIND OF INTIMACY—WITH YOURSELF, WITH OTHERS, AND WITH GOD.

Maybe there's a part of you that still grieves a path not taken, an opportunity missed, or a version of your life you once imagined. It can feel strange to offer compassion to that ache, especially when you're also grateful for what your life holds today. On one level, it may not make sense to feel both grief and gratitude. But on another, it's absolutely essential.

When you allow yourself to hold both love and sorrow together, you make space for a deeper kind of intimacy—with yourself, with others, and with God.

This is the paradox of repair: You become stronger not by denying what was lost, but by meeting it with compassion. As you turn toward past regrets or mistakes—not to dwell, but to reclaim—you cultivate an inner strength, vitality, and wisdom that is unshakable.

And it yields the fruit of a secure soul—one that is held through every change, every challenge, and every ache in Love.

REPAIRING WITH GOD

And then come the harder questions, the ones that may still live in broken pieces of your heart:

Where was God?

Why didn't God step in?

Why didn't God protect me from myself, or from other people?

When you've been hurt, barely survived, or clawed your way to a better place, God's love can feel . . . well, complicated. On one level, you may sense that God was the only One who helped you, and a place of gratitude lives there. And yet another part of you may be furious: *You could have stopped it.* Still another may feel numb or closed off: *I just can't deal with God.* Amid all this inner noise, it can be tempting to build a wall of self-reliance just to keep the turmoil at bay.

But these feelings need your care. They're the honest cries of your soul. Each one comes from a part of you trying to protect you in the only way it knows how. Each one is a bid for connection.

Because so often those inner responses toward God echo much older longings and disappointments: the hope that someone would step in, the ache for rescue, the need for a presence strong enough to hold your anger and steady enough to stay, even when you pull away.

And spiritual repair starts the same way all repair does: by learning to *recognize* what's rising inside you, and trusting that you are loved, even here.

You *recognize*:

I'm exhausted.

I'm angry.

I can't let go.

A part of me doesn't like God very much.

You return to Love, staying curious instead of condemning:

Of course you feel that way.

You've been hurt.

You're scared.

You're not sure how to trust.

And as you practice this sacred rhythm of connection, something new begins to form.

I've seen this in others, and I've lived it myself.

THE TRANSFORMATION OF THE CONTROLLER

When I look back at the twenty-seven-year-old version of me—the one buried in books, just before the panic attacks began—I can see now that she wasn't only wrestling with ideas. She was still reaching for God in the only way she knew how.

She stayed fiercely loyal, protective of God in much the same way she'd always felt protective of loved ones. For her, connection meant faithfulness, responsibility, and trying harder to keep it all together while quietly silencing her own needs. Don't get me wrong, faithfulness, loyalty, and responsbility are not bad things. They kept me anchored through many hard seasons.

But when pain surfaced that she didn't know how to hold, she tightened her grip instead of learning to let Love in.

This was my Inner Controller at work.

She believed, sincerely, that she could manage, override, or pray away the messiness of being human, including the loneliness, confusion, and fear. Longing became a liability. Needing help felt like weakness. She interpreted emotional pain as failure. She mistook a broken spirit for lack of willpower.[3]

From where I stand now, I can see what she could not then: not a woman in need of more effort or discipline, but one in need of *care*. Of presence. Of support.

And I see this pattern all the time, especially in women. Women who have learned to confess their pain instead of care for it. To repent of their needs instead of learning to tend to them with love.

The good news is this: When your Inner Controller is finally held in Love, she no longer has to manage your inner world all on her own. She doesn't disappear, nor does she get dismantled. Instead, she's honored. She's seen. She's *supported*.

And slowly, she begins to transform.

What once showed up as control matures into steadiness. What once felt like vigilance becomes discernment. What once worked relentlessly to keep everything from falling apart learns to rest—and to tend what has been entrusted to her with wisdom and restraint.

The Controller becomes the *Steward*.

Not the one who forces outcomes, but the one who watches over what matters. Not driven by fear of loss, but grounded in loving responsibility.

And from that place, your soul expands into a steadier kind of freedom—one where Love holds what you were never meant to hold alone.

Recognize: *I'm holding regret.*

Return: *I am loved, even here.*

CHAPTER 11

OPEN YOURSELF TO RISK

Taking risks is such a tricky yet necessary part of an integrated life.

The risk to love.

To contribute.

To serve.

To create.

Each risk requires vulnerability. Each one asks you to step forward without guarantees.

Risk is a hallmark feature of a secure soul.

Some of us take risks anxiously through pushing ourselves forward or bracing for rejection. Others avoid taking risks altogether. We pull back, telling ourselves we don't care. But a secure soul risks differently. Instead of trying to prove ourselves or shrink in self-protection, we learn to show up *whole,* humbly, freely, and with intention.

RISK IS A HALLMARK FEATURE OF A SECURE SOUL.

A secure soul risks from love, not for love.[1]

It's taken me decades to understand the difference.

THE COURAGE TO BE SEEN

I am an intensely private person. And yet I find myself with the strange conundrum of having a public platform.

Writing books? No problem. Podcasting? Great! I can labor over these endeavors from the privacy of my home, flannel shirt, no makeup, next to my two blissfully sleeping doodles. Research. Write. Revise. Never showing anyone the messy middle of the imperfections.

But put me under a spotlight or ask me to deliver on command, and it will draw out the very worst of my inner soul mountain.

On this particular day, I need to make a video to introduce my work to a sales team, because, well, you can't just disappear into the safety of your cave to *write* books. In the real world, you also have to *market* them, as in publicly.

So I put on my makeup and comb my hair. I try to look presentable. And under the harsh ring light, my phone propped up against a stack of books, pointing at me with its glaring camera eye, I find myself staring at a script that suddenly feels paper-thin.

And the noise inside my soul erupts.

My Inner Controller's grip clenches tight as she frantically writes and rewrites and overthinks and adjusts every single phrase.

The voice of my Inner Shadow is piercing and clear: *You're the worst at this. Why can't you be more like (fill in the blank here)? They make it seem so effortless! You* moron.

Meanwhile, the Young One inside—the one who typically brings the creativity and love and vitality—feels increasingly small. Her playful voice is lost deep within my inner soul mountain.

So I stop. Take a deep breath.

I lift my gaze and see the mountain, my ever-steady attachment tether, outside my window, beaming down like a gentle, loving mother.

And something in me shifts. *Is it possible for this to be* fun?

What a novel idea! How can I make this fun? And right then I decide to take the whole show outside, where I can feel more like myself. Out where the stream winds lazily past turkeys preening, and the cows chime in from behind them, utterly unimpressed.

Out here, my need for perfection loosens its grip. My soul can breathe again.

I set up my tripod right in the middle of our front field. I must have looked absurd to my rancher neighbors, who most definitely do not have tripods planted in the middle of their fields.

And as I get ready to hit record, I steady myself with one of my favorite Scriptures, lifting my eyes toward the mountain:

My soul finds rest in God alone.[2]

I turn toward my Inner Controller clamped down and gripping tight. I take a deep breath and give her a kind but firm look, as if to say, *I see you there; I see what you're doing.*

Almost immediately, I feel her step back, loosening her grip. *I'm sorry*, she seems to say. *I know all that pressure doesn't actually help.* My shoulders unclench. A little more space opens up inside.

Then I turn toward the harshness of my Inner Shadow. Again, a kind but firm look is all she needs. She, too, steps back, eyes sheepish. *I slipped again*, she admits penitently. *I'm sorry.*

It's okay, I tell her—silently, of course. (My neighbors would really start to wonder if I was doing all this out loud!) *I know you're trying to help.*

Then, as I turn back toward my tripod—feeling lighter, more spacious—I'm surprised by a new insight that rises within my soul.

This material is really good.

The sincerity stops me in my tracks. It isn't saccharine or sentimental. It's not some phony inner hype man. It feels like something rarer: a part of me simply naming what is *true.*

And I recognize the voice. It's coming from my Inner Shadow, the one who has long been my most ferocious inner eviscerater.

This is good material, she says again. *You've done good work here.*

And this simple naming feels completely true.

Not because it's perfect or beyond critique. But still, I believe her.

This Shadow-turned-Seer isn't offering reassurance. She's naming what is real.

And just as I begin to take in this shift, this unexpected kindness, another feeling rises from deep within, quiet but unmistakable:

I'm terrified to care.

THE RISK OF CARING

In that moment—standing in the field talking to myself with my iPhone perched on a tripod—I have an epiphany. I finally understand why my Inner Shadow has worked so hard to eviscerate me, and why my Inner Controller has strained so fiercely to perfect.

It's because I *care*.

I care deeply.

And it's terrifying to care.

Caring is risky.

Caring is vulnerable.

Sometimes we care, and something we've poured ourselves into doesn't turn out the way we hoped.

Sometimes we care about things we long for—and don't receive.

Sometimes we care, and the people we reach out to refuse our care.

It's easier to pretend something or someone—a project, a relationship, a calling—doesn't really matter. It's easier to protect yourself from disappointment before it even arrives. It's easier to hide behind overfunctioning or self-critique than to admit, deep within your soul, how much this actually matters to you.

I care about this relationship. I want to heal it.

I care about this work. This offering. I want this to go well. I hope this matters to someone.

It's vulnerable to care. It's far easier to lean into control or perfectionism, those familiar tactics that promise safety but keep us striving and distant. Or we retreat into cynicism or guardedness, those hidden ways we try to pretend we don't need much at all.

Because to care deeply is to risk. To open yourself to what you cannot control. And that kind of caring requires trust—trust that something larger, steadier, is holding you, even when you stumble or your efforts fail.

This is what a secure soul makes possible.

A secure soul gives us the courage to care without guaranteeing the outcome.

Think of a child trying to make a new friend. She lingers nearby, watching, rehearsing what she might say. When she feels securely held—when there's a steady, reliable presence in the background—she's more willing to take the risk. She reaches out. She tries again. She can even laugh when things don't go as planned.

A SECURE SOUL GIVES US THE COURAGE TO CARE WITHOUT GUARANTEEING THE OUTCOME.

That's how secure attachment works. *The confidence of being held gives rise to the courage to reach out.* That steady presence becomes an invisible tether that says, *You can risk caring. You can risk reaching out. No matter what happens, you are held.*

And if her efforts fail or if the moment falls flat, she can return to the arms of the one who loves her. She's comforted, steadied, reminded that the disappointment doesn't define her. And then, when she's ready, she heads back out again.

That's how resilience is built: *not by avoiding failure or rejection, but by being held through it. Not by never risking care, but by knowing there is love to return to when the risk hurts.*

When you allow yourself to care, and when you trust that you are being lovingly held no matter the outcome, you are freer to step out into vulnerable spaces. You risk failing. You risk disappointment. You risk feeling foolish.

But you also risk connection. You risk meaning. You risk love.

DEVELOPING AN ANCHOR WITHIN

An inner anchor doesn't mean you never wobble. It means you have *a center you can return to when you do*. Over time, the different parts of your soul mountain learn to trust you, and the One who holds them, until a sense of steadiness feels as close as your next conscious breath.

When you notice the Controller rising inside you, it's often a signal of a moment when you care deeply. She arrives with urgency and resolve, convinced that if she can just manage this well enough, perfect it enough, hold it tightly enough, she can protect you from disappointment.

Instead of pushing her away or letting her take over, try pausing.

Breathe.

Gently remind her, *You don't have to carry this alone.*

Sometimes that simple acknowledgment is enough for her shoulders, and yours, to soften. Control gives way to *care.* Pressure gives way to *trust.* And in that shift, the Controller begins to exhale, as she remembers her truer role.

She once again becomes the Steward.

The Steward knows that caring requires responsibility, but not a tight grip. She holds risk with humility, tending what is hers to tend while releasing what is not. She understands that showing up well matters, but outcomes cannot be forced. She learns to *lean into love* rather than try to secure it.

The Shadow responds to risk differently. When caring feels too vulnerable, she warns you not to hope too much. Not to invest. Not to open yourself up to the possibility of disappointment. Sometimes she criticizes. Sometimes she numbs. Sometimes she pulls you away from what matters before it can hurt you.

When she shows up, she also needs your compassion instead of contempt. You might say to her, *I see you. It's scary to care. It makes sense that you want to find relief.*

Then do something small and steady. For example, you might take a walk, place a hand over your heart, drink a glass of water, or step outside where you can breathe more freely. These simple gestures remind her that safety doesn't come from shutting down but from *staying connected.*

Little by little, she learns that it's okay to remain present. And from that grounded place, her longing for escape softens into wisdom.

She remembers she's the Seer. The Seer doesn't eviscerate hope or inflate fear. Instead, she tells the truth with steadiness. She helps you see what's real—what's worth caring about, what's possible, and what's not—without collapsing into cynicism or fantasy.

As the Steward and Seer take on new roles, something subtle but important shifts inside you. You're no longer driven by urgency or fear, nor pulled entirely by longing. Instead, you begin to sense a different kind of strength. You begin to trust that your soul can stay present with desire without being swept away by it, and stay present with fear without shutting down.

This is the beginning of discernment.

A secure soul doesn't rush into every risk, nor does it shrink back from all of them. It listens. It notices. It waits until your whole soul—not just one part—is present and engaged. Decisions come from a more integrated place, shaped by honesty, capacity, and care.

You begin to sense a deeper truth:

I don't have to risk to be loved. I can risk because I already am.

The willingness to make yourself vulnerable becomes an expression of trust.

Each small act of tuning in with honesty and care weaves a deeper inner web of connection, a secure holding place within.

That inner anchor doesn't remove the vulnerability of bringing your authentic gifts and longings into the world. But it offers a way to stay connected *within the vulnerability*—open, grounded, and whole.

It's the confidence of a soul that no longer waits for perfect circumstances to feel okay.

It's the deep knowing: *Even here, even now, I am held.*

And as you take these steps over time, you start to experience what secure attachment feels like from the inside out, the steady practice of learning to trust *within* yourself.

Not through control. Not through perfection. Through loving presence.

ANCHORED BY IMAGINATION

We were never meant to risk alone. Even as you learn to anchor within, there are moments when insecurity strikes, when you feel exposed, or when shame draws near. In those moments, you need reminders of love. Sometimes those reminders come from beyond you. And sometimes, they come from within.

This is where the power of memory and imagination comes in. Through imagination, you can call to mind the face of a person who has held steady for you in the past. You can imagine a place that once grounded you, or even a part of yourself. Imagination allows you to remember what safety feels like, and to reenter it, even when you're alone.

When you allow yourself to contemplate goodness—to picture love, steadiness, and safety—you make room for God to meet you in the places your logic or self-talk can't reach.[3]

Not that long ago, I was presenting at a conference alongside several well-known authors and speakers, each one far more seasoned at commanding big stages than I am. It was a risk. And normally, my soul would be chaotic leading up to such settings. But this time I was steady. Grounded. I had done the work internally.

And then came a twist.

The night before I was scheduled to speak, all four speakers were seated side by side for a book signing after the first day's events. My heart sank. I knew what was about to happen.

Sure enough, lines began to form quickly in front of the other, more well-known speakers—long, winding lines of people eager to meet them. And there I sat, the one they didn't know yet. I looked out at the open space in front of me: empty. Completely, painfully *empty.*

The kind of empty where you suddenly wish for an invisibility cloak. The kind where your cheeks burn, your chest tightens, and your inner critic hisses, *See? You don't belong here. All that work you've done? It doesn't even matter.* For a moment, shame rose up in me like a wave. Then I caught it—*the familiar bid for connection.*

My mind scrambled. I couldn't go anywhere. I couldn't phone a friend. And then I remembered.

Recognize: *I'm disconnected.*

Return: *I am loved.*

I took a deep breath. I asked God to steady me. And almost instantly, an image rose in my mind, a scene from what I'd left back home: my husband reading out on our front porch, as the mountain watched over him, and our two scruffy doodles begging him to throw the ball for them. I instantly felt calmer, loved, secure. Then, I thought, *I can't wait to tell him about this when I get home.*

I imagined how I would tell him about this moment and how we would laugh. And how he would reassure me, *But you hadn't even spoken yet! Of course they didn't know you.* But it wasn't his words or logic that steadied me—it was the connectedness. The knowing that he would get it, that he would see the humor in it, that *I wasn't alone.*

And just like that, I smiled. Literally. Right there as I sat in my chair. What could have been a moment of humiliation turned into an inside joke I couldn't wait to share.

Later that night, as I reviewed my notes for the next day's talk, I returned to my imagination, gathering the different parts of me right there in my hotel room. I pictured each of them sitting in a circle, with me at the center—calm, present, and steady—helping each one do their best. Instead of spiraling into self-sabotage or anxious striving, I set a simple intention:

Let's have fun with this. It doesn't have to be perfect. Let's just share what we actually know, the very work we're learning to live.

One by one, each part of me relaxed into that invitation.

And I felt a deeper sense of inner connectedness take hold.

The next morning, as we sang "It Is Well with My Soul," just before I was set to take the stage, I reconnected one more time.

I see my Controller-turned-Steward to the left, flannel shirt, ponytail tight. I let her know: *You've worked so hard.*

I'm proud of you. You know this material. Let go of the prep and enjoy sharing what you've learned.

Then I turn to my Shadow-turned-Seer, perched there to my right. But before I can even say a word, she pipes in with her newly discovered knack for saying what's true: *This is good material. You're ready, coach.*

Finally, I place my hand over my heart and connect with the Young One deep inside. *It was never your job to earn love. To prove your worth. You are already so deeply loved.* And just like that, she crawls up on the very top of my shoulders so that she can get a better view. She is delighted to be here with me. She feels safe with me.

I am safe with me.

Just then, I hear the conference director introduce me, and I walk on stage brimming over with a childlike sense of wonder. I can feel every part of me *with me*—steady, vibrant, grateful. Connected.

I am having *fun*.

A few moments into the talk, I cannot find the projector image, the one displaying my visuals. I freeze for half a second, then spot it, way above the stage lights. Without thinking, I point and say gleefully, "Hey—there are the images I made!"

The audience bursts out laughing, and I am laughing with them. I relax into what becomes a delightful conversation among a small gathering of a thousand friends.

Afterward, I am so deeply happy and proud within myself. Not because it was perfect. But because *I stayed with myself.*

Every part of me came along. And because of that, I

was free to be fully present—with the audience, and with myself.

THE JOY OF TAKING A RISK

Who, or what, helps you feel safe enough to exhale?

It might be a person, a place, or even a memory.

And it might also be a version of yourself, the steadier self you're learning to inhabit.

THAT'S WHAT AN INNER ANCHOR OF CONNECTION DOES—IT STEADIES YOU. IT KEEPS YOU FROM SPIRALING INTO SHAME OR GRASPING FOR CONTROL OR PERFECTION.

These are your *attachment tethers*, the reminders that you don't have to take a risk alone. And they live inside you, even when they're far away.

You might visualize the face of someone who loves you without condition.

You might picture God steadying you with loving presence.

Or you might imagine yourself turning gently toward the more tender parts of your own soul and meeting them with the same care you always longed for.

That's what an inner anchor of connection does—it steadies you. It keeps you from spiraling into shame or grasping for control or perfection. The safety of that inner belonging frees you to show up imperfectly but *wholly yourself*.[4]

When connection holds you from within,

- the Controller doesn't have to carry all the pressure anymore,
- the Shadow doesn't have to lash out in fear, and
- the Young One is free to bring her sense of childlike wonder, play, and curiosity.

With every risk comes an invitation—a moment when you exhale and learn to trust within yourself. Whether the risk ends in wild success or in a raucous failure that you can later laugh (or cry) about with a friend, the secure soul doesn't measure success by applause or outcome but by integrity.

Did I show up as myself? Did I stay connected to Love?

This is the rhythm of secure living:

You take a risk.

You return to Love.

You rest.

Your soul can exhale because you're no longer performing for safety. You're *participating in love*.

Secure love doesn't remove risk, nor does it promise certain outcomes. Instead, secure love steadies you for it.

It whispers, *You're safe enough to show up. You're held enough to try. You can care deeply and still be okay, no matter what happens.*

As I sit back at my desk, remembering the conference and the empty line in front of me—and the way I walked onto that stage so filled up inside that next morning—I smile. I shake my head.

I cared.

I took a risk.

I wobbled.

I returned to Love.

And I risked again.

I can't believe how far my soul has come.

Outside my window stands the mountain. It's the same one that watched over me as a young girl crying out to God; the one I drove toward as a teenager, belting out my angst to '80s hair bands; and the one that reminded me just the other week to *have fun* with my work.

> I lift up my eyes to the mountains—
> where does my help come from?
> My help comes from the LORD,
> the Maker of heaven and earth.
>
> *(Ps. 121:1–2)*

And something lands deep within me, not a new thought, but a deeper knowing.

As steady as that mountain has been throughout every season of my life, it was never the source. It was always the sign.

A reflection. A witness. A way God makes loving presence visible.

It was always Love.

Every person. Every place. Every sacred stretch of sky that has steadied your soul along the way—each one has always been a signpost pointing your heart, again and again, back to Love.

Recognize: *I'm scared to take a risk.*

Return: *I am loved, even here.*

CHAPTER 12

DISCOVER WHERE YOUR SOUL FINDS A HOME

As Wendell Berry wrote so beautifully, "The soil is the great connector of lives, the source and destination of it all."[1]

Our souls are shaped not only by the people who have held us but by the places that have held our lives. It might be a stretch of highway, the sound of a train at night, or the familiar curve of a driveway. It might be a skyline or a mountain ridge. Each one bears witness to the different seasons of our lives.

We live in a world of constant movement. Addresses change. Roles shift. People come and go. Even when we stay put, the world around us rarely does.

A secure soul learns how to live within this rhythm. It knows how to settle without getting stuck, and how to move through seasons without losing its center.

Often, it learns this through moments of unexpected recognition—when something familiar meets us again and reminds us where, and with whom, we belong.

WHERE I AM KNOWN

I'm attending a group fitness class at the local YMCA with my eighty-three-year-old dad, the same YMCA where I would go to swim, run around the track with my mom, and watch my dad play handball as a kid.

To my surprise, the Young One is present with me here, the one who suddenly showed up on the late-night prayer walk in London. I had wondered if she only showed up on faraway trips.

And yet here she is, over the moon to be warming up for a morning "gentle strengthening" class with about a dozen eighty-year-olds—walking in circles, waving our arms, and working on balance, all while listening to Heart belt out its '80s hit classic: "*Never, never, never run away!*"[2]

My mom and dad have recently moved back to Wyoming after spending the past two decades in New England heading up a ministry, and the transition has been hard on them. I want to support my dad as he bravely joins the local Y and steps back into the community. I offer to pick him up in our old, boxy Ford Escape and go with him to his first day of class.

But I am beginning to realize that my being here isn't only for *him*.

I'm walking next to my dad in this circle, and I feel a strange sense of urgency to stay close to him. The Young One's presence inside me is unmistakable, so tender and alive.

To be honest, I need a real workout this morning—something more suited for my fifty-year-old body, which isn't exactly nimble anymore but still wants more than what's asked of us in this class designed for seniors.

But the Young One inside me doesn't want to leave him.

It feels like to leave his side is to pull apart something that feels so connected inside me, as if I'm a little girl again, basking in the safety of his presence.

I gently peel myself away from my dad's side, and step into the room next door, where I hop on the treadmill to get my own workout in while he finishes his class. But I can't ignore her, this tender presence that has followed me here. I thank her for letting me leave the other room, and I ask what it was about walking with my dad that touched her so deeply.

Images flood my mind. One memory in particular.

I'm about eight years old, walking with my dad from the small Ford dealership he runs with my grandfather to the Hallmark gift store a few blocks away on the corner of Main and Loucks. We're going to pick out a birthday card for my mom.

We cross Main Street, which feels like our version of the local Times Square, bustling with activity. My dad waves and greets nearly everyone we pass. He is warm and winsome. I feel like a tiny queen just to be by his side.

At the Hallmark store, we pick out the card for my mom. I stop to stare at the miniature gnome figurines in the glass cabinet next to the checkout register. I am mesmerized by their different expressions, their different ways of being in their little gnome world.

At the register, my dad realizes he's forgotten his wallet. He smacks his forehead with exaggerated flair. "What a doofus!" he says, laughing, completely unbothered. The store clerk laughs with him. "That's okay, Willard. You can drop the money by later." He thanks her, and we head back to the dealership with the birthday card in hand.

As we wait at the crosswalk, we are both giddy with laughter. We love that the cashier let him leave without paying for the card, and we can't wait to bring the money back. I feel proud to be with him. Proud that the clerk trusts him. Proud to be his tiny partner on this errand. We are bound by invisible threads of love. I love walking next to my dad.

Back on my treadmill at the YMCA, I'm teary-eyed.

But it's not just him I've missed.

I've missed being near him *here*—in this place, this small town in Wyoming, twenty miles south of the Montana border. This place at the base of the Bighorn Mountains. This place where my dad was raised by my grandparents in a house just a few miles down the street from the house where he and my mom raised me.

There's something powerful about being with someone you love in the environment that shaped both of you. It's not just geography. And it's deeper than attachment. It's *belonging*.

Later, my dad and I walk out of the Y together.

We run into Missy, one of my childhood-turned-adult friends. She hasn't seen my dad since we were in high school together, since the surprise birthday party my dad threw for me on my eighteenth birthday.

"Hi, Mr. Cook!" Missy says, grinning as she gives him a hug.

His eyes light up. He's seen. He's known. He is *delighted*.

And I'm weeping inside as I fight to keep the tears from spilling over and onto my face.

It's such a small moment—my dad being recognized by someone who knew him decades ago. But it brings tears to my eyes because it reminds me of something I'd almost forgotten: what it feels like to be *placed*. To be located. To be part of a living, breathing web of familiarity, where even a quick trip to the YMCA carries echoes of the past.

THE GEOGRAPHY OF BELONGING

That morning at the YMCA stirred something deeper than just attachment to my dad. It reminded me of the broader tethering I once knew, the kind that comes from being known by a *place*.

Place is a kind of attachment figure, secure yet changing, offering both the safety of belonging and the steadiness of something larger than ourselves. Psychologists call this *place attachment*—the bond between our inner life and the outer world that has witnessed it. A familiar landscape, a home, or a school building. The rooms that carried your laughter and your tears, the neighborhood block that helped raise you.

Whatever the landscape, this place becomes a kind of mirror for your soul, a quiet witness to who you were and who you're still becoming.

For me, that mirror has always been this small town nestled in the shadow of the mostly undiscovered Bighorn Mountains in northern Wyoming. I didn't realize how deeply that landscape had held and formed my soul until I left.

The geography here carries a particular kind of wisdom with boundaries and expansiveness held together. The mountains offer a towering sense of containment to the west of our town, even as the vast plains—nothing but sagebrush, cattle, and sky—invite a spaciousness that stretches for miles in every other direction.

When you're in my hometown, *this is it.* There's no "better mall" across town, no "other" movie theater or second hospital just a few exits away. What's here is *what's here.* Sheridan County is blissfully not the billionaire wilderness that Jackson Hole and Bozeman, Montana—what we call "Boze-Angeles"—have become. That's why it comes with a warning sign: *Please visit! Don't stay!*

I used to see all that isolation as limitation. I couldn't wait to leave when I went off to college back East, and then on to live in several different cities over a decade, each one scattered across the country. But now I see this land that held me for my first eighteen years as *formation.* When there's nowhere else to run, you learn to stay. You learn to know a place—and let it know you. That kind of rootedness imprints something steady in the soul.

Whether your landscape was a crowded city block or an endless plain, we all carry some internalized version of place, a kind of inner geography that taught us how to feel *located*, with all the good and hard that comes with that.

Where are the places that have brought your soul a sense of familiarity—where, even now, your breath deepens and your eyes can finally rest?

Maybe it's the stretch of water that once calmed you, and still does, or rolling hills that have held you in different seasons of your life.

Maybe it's a sidewalk you've walked a thousand times, the hum of a city block at dusk, or a park bench where you once felt less alone.

Psychologists call these *small attachments*: the ordinary bonds that make us feel less alone. The contours of a home you know by heart. The barista who remembers your order. The mountain ridge or skyline etched into memory. These are the quiet tethers that remind us we belong.

Spiritually speaking, these same attachments become *sacred tethers*. They're earthly reflections of divine nearness through every season of your life.

The mountain that still stands, even when your marriage is crumbling.

The sunrise that greets you after a night of tears.

The familiar place that holds you steady, even when everything else has changed.

These physical, tangible anchors give voice to the reality that *God is still here*.

The psalmist knew this truth well. Again and again, the Psalms point to creation as a reminder of God's nearness: "The heavens declare the glory of God; the skies proclaim the work of his hands" (Ps. 19:1).

For the psalmist, mountains, skies, rivers, and fields weren't just scenery. They were embodied signs of a God who is always present.

These sacred tethers aren't fleeting moments. They're deep signals of Divine Love—reminders that God's presence is not confined to heaven but alive in the very texture of this world.

FOR THE PSALMIST, MOUNTAINS, SKIES, RIVERS, AND FIELDS WEREN'T JUST SCENERY. THEY WERE EMBODIED SIGNS OF A GOD WHO IS ALWAYS PRESENT.

The places that hold us, both kindly and imperfectly, become essential parts of how our souls are formed.

And when the landscape around us shifts, it's essential that we tend to the landscape within. To pause long enough to notice what feels uprooted, what needs care, and what still holds steady.

Because when too much change happens without that inner tending, the soul can lose its footing.

WHEN THE GROUND SHIFTS

When the ground beneath us shifts, we often move too quickly through change without tending to the transition itself. Think of a plant moved from one bed of soil to another. Aboveground, it might look just fine. But below the surface, its roots are fragile. Without extra care, nourishment, and time, the plant struggles to take hold. The same is true for us. Even changes made for growth can leave us more unmoored if our inner root system isn't supported.

Each move, loss, or life transition—relocating to a new place, learning how to live inside a changed relationship, launching a child into a new season—asks something of us beneath the surface. When we move through these moments without enough support, parts of us struggle to keep our footing.

Different parts of your soul respond differently when the ground shifts. For example, one part of you might embrace the change while another grieves what you're leaving behind. A friend recently texted me photos on the day her youngest of three children started college. She was both excited about her newfound freedom and mourning the loss of having children at home. Even healthy transitions can carry an ache, because the landscape of daily life has shifted.

THE GOOD NEWS IS THAT YOU CAN LEARN TO SECURE YOUR SOUL THROUGH TRANSITION.

The good news is that you can learn to secure your soul through transition.

Our task isn't to force ourselves to adapt quickly, but to tend what's tender within us—to pause and say: *I see you. I know this is hard. We don't have to rush.*

It starts by noticing the different bids for connection that arise in seasons of change. It might be the anxious part that struggles when routines shift, the grieving part that longs for what was, or the capable part that tries to hold it all together. All of them need to know that you are with them, and that God is with them too.

Often, the Controller steps forward during transition. She likes familiarity and predictability. When the ground shifts, she works harder, barreling through change, head down, determined to keep things steady. Her bids for connection often show up like this:

- She tightens her grip, doubling down on planning and productivity.
- She equates safety with sameness, remaining skeptical of new rhythms, relationships, or environments.
- She overrides emotion with action, mistaking lengthy to-do lists for resilience.
- She relies on her age-old mantra: *I'm fine!*

At her core, the Controller is loyal. She wants to keep you safe. What she needs most is reassurance that slowing down won't lead to collapse and that she, too, can be held.

When you notice her striving, you might invite her to downshift. Not necessarily to stop altogether, but to pace herself. Transition is rarely a sprint. It's more often a long, uneven road that requires patience and rest along the way.

The Shadow often shows up differently. She's the one who tends to sense when real change is needed. She names the truth and pushes for movement. But she can also rush ahead, burning bridges or running away instead of allowing for the slow, patient work of wisdom.

I've seen this in my own life. When I took time off from graduate school after I started having panic attacks, my newly liberated Inner Shadow surged forward impulsively. I didn't just gently learn new rhythms, I uprooted my entire life, moving far away from friends, family, and school into a tiny garden apartment in Los Angeles. That season was beautiful in many ways, but when I look back, I see how my Shadow had overcorrected. I didn't need to scorch the earth. I needed time, care, and gentler shifts.

The Shadow carries a paradox: She's both the truth-teller and the flight risk. She longs for freedom, but she needs to know that *freedom can coexist with care*. Her bids for connection sound like this:

- A restlessness that urges you to leave, quit, or change everything all at once
- A voice that speaks in extremes—*I'm done!*—even if she doesn't know what comes next
- A craving for space to breathe, away from anything that feels constricting
- An urge to push against others, as a way of testing who will stay

At her core, the Shadow is authentic. She wants to be known as she really is—fiery, honest, and alive. What she needs most is compassion, not shame. Reassurance that her longing won't be dismissed and that she doesn't have to rush to be taken seriously.

When each of these parts of you is met with care, something begins to shift. The Controller loosens her grip and softens into your inner Steward, helping you honor what you're leaving behind while creating enough structure to move forward with care. The Shadow slows her pace and finds her footing as the Seer, helping you tell the truth about what needs to change without burning everything down.

And the Young One within you feels safer to emerge. She no longer has to brace herself against abrupt change or relentless forward motion. She can bring curiosity, tenderness, and a sense of hope and wonder into the transition, trusting that she will be tended, not rushed.

This is how we tend the soul when the ground shifts: not by forcing growth, but by offering presence. By staying close enough to notice what's still fragile. By trusting that with time, care, and love, new roots can take hold again.

THE DEEPLY ROOTED SOUL

When this kind of inner tending becomes familiar, change begins to feel different. Not easier, exactly, but steadier. More grounded.

Life no longer swings between white-knuckled willpower and the urge to escape. Instead, your inner world starts to find a rhythm. The Controller-turned-Steward brings continuity. The Shadow-turned-Seer brings discernment. One offers containment, while the other invites movement. Together, they create the conditions for rootedness, helping you build a life that is both stable and alive, both rooted and free.

LIFE NO LONGER SWINGS BETWEEN WHITE-KNUCKLED WILLPOWER AND THE URGE TO ESCAPE.

Practically speaking, that kind of integration looks like this:

- You create space for rest without guilt.
- You take a risk, but not a reckless one.
- You speak an honest truth, but with kindness.
- You allow yourself to be seen in a new way, but without abandoning your convictions.

When control and freedom meet in care, you begin to experience what secure attachment within yourself feels like—a grounded confidence that says, *I can hold steady, even as things change.*

I witnessed the most vivid example of this through my mother-in-law. At nineteen, she and her young husband fled Lithuania on bicycles as Russia invaded during World War II. They lived in displaced-persons camps for five years before eventually settling in the United States, where she gave birth to my husband in a Lithuanian borough of New York City. She had left behind her home, her family, her language—everything she knew. And yet from the moment I met her at her apartment, where she now lived near Boston, I recognized a woman who was *deeply at home*. It wasn't because she forgot the past, nor because she clung to it, but because she found ways to bring her home into her present.

To this day, my kids' favorite holiday meals are *kugelis*, *vėrinukai*, and the Christmas Eve table of *Kūčios*. Her greeting, *Labas*, still lives among us. Through food, language, story, and ritual, she wove the old world into the new, transforming loss into a new kind of belonging.

In her, I saw what it looks like when both strength and longing live in harmony—the grit of the Controller meeting the vitality of the Shadow. Structure and movement, memory and renewal, order and imagination all working together under the steady gaze of Love.

AN ECOSYSTEM OF ATTACHMENT

The beauty of this inner work is that it doesn't stay inside you. It reshapes how you attach to the world around you.

You no longer cling to one patch of earth, nor do you need to sever ties in order to move on. Instead, you learn to honor the places that have shaped you, staying connected without becoming rigid, staying honest without closing off. Over time, you gather pieces of different landscapes within yourself, building an inner terrain shaped by the calm of one season, the courage of another, the wonder of yet another.

You learn that it's safe to venture out—and to come back again. That you can explore new terrain without losing your footing. When you integrate the ground that holds you, your soul can stretch, risk, and grow.

The truth is that God has created a whole ecosystem of loving attachment—numerous, interconnected ways for us to experience nearness, belonging, and a sense of being held every single day.

I think of this ecosystem as consisting of *place*, *people*, and *parts*, all held together by loving Presence.

Place is the soil, rich with memory, landscape, and embodied presence. It grounds you in what is real, settling you in your body and in the created world. Even in your most fragile moments, the ground beneath you still bears witness: The tree still stands in winter; the mountain remains through the storm; the walls still hold, even when your heart is breaking.

People are the roots that intertwine with yours, sometimes steady, sometimes tangled, always shaping how you grow. Through relationships—with friends, parents, mentors, family members, a spouse or significant other—you learn what love feels like. These connections can wound, disappoint, confuse, or break trust. And yet, when someone truly sees you, stays with you, or mirrors your worth, those moments stitch ruptured parts of your soul back together.

The *parts within your own soul* form the hidden root system of this living network, the interior channels that carry memory and emotion. They hold what you have loved and what you have lost, what has nourished you and what has wounded you. And when these parts are met with curiosity, compassion, and care, they help restore trust, keeping you rooted in what is *good and true*, even as the world around you changes.

Through it all flows the stream of God's loving presence—the living water nourishing everything seen and unseen. It moves through every root and branch, every tender shoot reaching for the light, and every place that has been cracked or broken, sustaining all of us through what remains and what changes.

As you grow more attuned to that flow, you begin to see how Love has been weaving it all together, this grand story of your life. Every person, every place, every part of your soul becomes part of that larger story. You are also woven into the story of others. The ground beneath your feet, the faces that have met you, the memories that rise unbidden—all of it is held in God.

And while *home* in this life can feel elusive, every longing for connectedness, every ache and every signal points us to what's possible: a deeper anchoring. A way of carrying *home* within you, wherever you go.

Home is no longer only outside you. Home is also being formed within.

And from that home, you begin to move through the world differently.

Not grasping.

Not escaping.

Not collapsing into someone else.

But grounded. Present. Whole.

Recognize: *I'm untethered.*

Return: *I am loved, even here.*

CHAPTER 13

ENJOY CLOSENESS WITHOUT COLLAPSE

After all this inner work, we arrive at a final question—the question most conversations about attachment *start* with:

What does a secure soul look like in relationships with other people?

It's one thing to feel anchored within yourself: to rest in divine Love, to know your worth, to repair within, to learn to take risks, and to internalize a sense of place. But it's another to bring that secure grounding into the messy, beautiful realm of human relationships.

Because this is where the work is tested—in marriage and friendship, in community and conversation, in all the places where you encounter people whose inner soul mountains look nothing like your own. Their inner terrain carries different textures, different stories, different areas of wounding.

Here's the good news: As you've cultivated a secure soul within, you've *already learned* the core skills required to nurture healthy relationships with other people.

- You've learned how to stay connected to a part of you without collapsing into it.
- You've learned how to approach with compassion and curiosity, instead of criticism or judgment.
- You've seen how the different parts of your soul can work together, each one distinct yet joined together by the Love who holds them.

And all that *inner* work becomes the seedbed for every *outer* relationship that you have.

The same rhythm of connectedness you've practiced inside yourself now extends outward to friends, family members, colleagues, and communities. You begin to recognize that what you've cultivated within—compassion, curiosity, containment—is exactly what makes real connection, real intimacy, possible.

When your soul is secure, you experience the fruit of inner integrity, what psychologists call *self-differentiation*. You can remain grounded in your own experience, beliefs, and feelings without needing to control, manage, or earn approval from someone else.

FRIEND DATE

There comes a moment when you realize something a little unsettling: If you want friends, you're going to have to risk something.

That's what happened to me.

Newly married, and finally settled into a new life in Boston, I realized I needed to figure out how to make friends—real, on-the-ground friends.

Part of me immediately recoiled at this idea. I was still recovering from years of overfunctioning. In the past, I knew how to be the listener, the steady one. But if I wasn't careful, I'd overextend, then eventually disappear when the closeness became too much.

I didn't want to repeat that pattern.

So when I noticed a few women around town, women I'd met briefly on the sidelines of the soccer field or seen at our local church, I felt both drawn and intimidated.

One evening, at an outdoor concert, I spotted several of them standing together. And without thinking, I hid. Literally. I ducked behind a food truck and pretended I hadn't seen them.

Later, chagrined with myself, I reflected on what that impulse was all about, and I could feel the familiar inner pressure. First, the vigilant voice of my Inner Controller:

Keep it tight.

Stay guarded, not exposed.

Don't give them anything to judge.

And then the Shadow put her foot on the gas. *Run!*

But something steadier in me knew *this is the growth*

edge—the place where connection asks more than self-protection.

So I gave it another try. I took a risk and reached out.

A quick email, simple and unpolished.

I've admired the volunteer work you're doing. Would you want to get coffee?

Pressing "send" felt like a small death to some part of me. I breathed through it.

As we set the time, I remembered what I'd learned when I started dating later in life: Start small. Coffee, not dinner. Clear beginning and ending. No promises. No pressure. Just presence.

And so here we are, sitting across from one another with mugs between us.

Almost immediately, I feel myself slipping into familiar territory—asking thoughtful questions, drawing her out, keeping the focus on her. This is how I stay safe. People generally enjoy talking about themselves, and I'm genuinely curious about them. It usually works.

Until she pauses and turns the questions back toward me.

"So," she said, "what's brought you to this point in your life?"

I take another breath.

I don't want to overshare. But I don't want to hide either. So I offer a few honest pieces—not as a test, exactly. More like an opening. A way of showing just enough to see what happens.

She doesn't flinch. She listens. She doesn't reassure, nor does she brush aside what I share. She simply takes it in.

I notice this.

And then comes the moment when I usually overperform, when I sense the need to secure the connection. To suggest a follow-up. To make a plan. To reassure both of us that this meant something.

I think of that old *Friends* episode where Chandler can't stop himself from saying, "I'll give you a call!" after a date, before he knows if he means it.[1] I smile inwardly and let myself pause.

"I've really enjoyed this," I say. "Thank you for making the time."

She says the same. No promises. No overstatement. Just honesty.

We stand, hug briefly, and part ways.

Later, walking to my car, I notice something surprising. I feel steady. Not elated. Not anxious. Just grounded.

That was it.

We connected. Nothing was demanded. Nothing was forced. Whatever might, or might not, grow from that encounter would unfold in its own time.

But something else had already shifted.

I trusted myself. I stayed present with her without abandoning myself. I let connection be spacious and gradual rather than pushing for it.

THIS IS WHAT A SECURE SOUL MAKES POSSIBLE: NOT THE ABSENCE OF FEAR, BUT THE CONFIDENCE THAT I CAN STAY WITH MYSELF, EVEN AS I STAY OPEN TO ANOTHER.

And I realize this is what a secure soul makes possible: not the absence of fear, but the confidence that I can stay with myself, even as I stay open to another.

LABORATORIES OF LOVE

Every relationship, from the deepest bond to the briefest encounter, becomes an invitation to practice what you've been learning all along—the rhythm of recognition and return.

Often, it's not the big moments that reveal an inner bid, but the small ones:

- A passing comment from a friend
- A child's eye roll
- A spouse's silence
- A colleague's tone
- An urge to please before anyone asks

These are the everyday laboratories of love.

In these ordinary moments, something inside us stirs up. Old wounds and familiar patterns surface. For example, we feel the urge to control, avoid, self-blame, or please. Not because we're failing, but because these relationships matter.

Beneath the surface of even the tiniest interactions, often lies a familiar ache:

Do I belong here?

Am I worthy of respect?

Can I stay connected without losing myself?

These questions don't necessarily disappear as we grow. They follow us into new seasons and new relationships, echoing the same longing for safety and connection that took shape in our earliest bonds.

A secure soul doesn't silence these questions or rush

to answer them. It recognizes them as *bids for connection* pointing us back to the parts of ourselves that need care and back to the Love that holds steady.

When you learn to meet these moments within yourself, something subtle begins to change. Instead of reacting to secure the relationship prematurely or prove your worth, you begin to pause and stay present. You respond from a deeper ground.

You stop shrinking to stay connected or overextending to stay safe.

You no longer need to defend yourself or overexplain.

Instead, security begins to show up in the fruit of your integrity.

And this is where the work begins to move beyond you.

As you grow steadier inside, you become less reactive to the inner movements of others. You can notice *their* bids for connection—their fear, their withdrawal, their need to be seen—without absorbing them or trying to manage them.

And something remarkable happens: You grow strong enough to hold space not only for your own inner life but also for the inner worlds of others.

A SECURE BASE FOR OTHERS

This is how the work of *inner attachment* ripens into *relational maturity*, a living ecosystem of love and safety that begins within you and flows outward to others, even as it continues to nourish you in return.

The more you learn to honor the anxious, avoidant,

protective, and tender parts within you, the more you can honor those same parts in others. You begin to recognize that every person you meet carries their own internal map of love, each soul shaped by joys and wounds, defenses and desires.

You don't need or expect perfection, nor do you gloss over real issues.

You no longer give trust away carelessly, nor do you withhold it out of fear.

Instead, you connect with *discernment*, grounded in the trust you've built with your own inner world and with God.

Here's the paradox of relational maturity: *You can trust others more freely precisely because you've learned to first show up for your own soul.*

As your inner world becomes more anchored, your relationships begin to feel different—not because the people around you have changed, but because *you* have. You no longer approach connection from a place of urgency or self-protection. You can stay present without taking over and stay connected without losing yourself.

HERE'S THE PARADOX OF RELATIONAL MATURITY: YOU CAN TRUST OTHERS MORE FREELY PRECISELY BECAUSE YOU'VE LEARNED TO FIRST SHOW UP FOR YOUR OWN SOUL.

From that steadier ground, relational maturity becomes possible:

You can let others grow without needing to control how.

You can hold space for both their needs and your own.

You can maintain boundaries and still stay connected.

You can honor difference without feeling threatened.

You can trust that Love will hold what you can't.

This inner steadiness begins to reshape the relational field around you. Others feel it. Not because you are managing them, but because you are no longer managing yourself against them.

When your soul is secure, you become a steady presence in the lives of others. You become the kind of person who helps create safety simply by being safe within yourself.

That's the gift of maturity: You learn to love without consuming, to stay connected without control, and to hold space for difference without needing to dominate or disappear.

And over time, this same posture of secure love moves into the wider world—into friendships, communities, and even conversations where beliefs or values diverge.

LOVE ACROSS DIFFERENCES

My friend Missy, the same one who recognized my dad at the YMCA, is an atheist. She's also one of my longest-standing friends, someone who has traveled through incredibly formative seasons of my life.

Both of us had found ourselves newly back in our hometown at the start of the pandemic, the unexpected gift of the burgeoning era of remote work. We started taking long walks through the same streets we'd once roamed as kids.

There's nothing quite like being with your inner sixteen-year-old *in the presence of someone who knew you when you were sixteen.* It's jarring, disorienting, and healing all at once. It's a portal into the past, even as you are connected in the present, offering a kind of embodied attachment encounter that feels almost extinct these days outside of a therapist's office.

During those miles, Missy and I retraced our lives, moving through old neighborhoods, familiar landmarks, and the shared geography of our growing up. We passed the high school track, where Missy shined; our friend Gretchen's house, the one who had all the good parties (the ones I wasn't allowed to go to); and the schoolyard, where the boy had seen my bloodstained checkered pants.

As we walked, it felt like moving through old layers of ourselves, as we touched on places that once held so much weight but no longer defined us in the same way.

It was there, as we walked through the schoolyard, that she told me about a boy we'd gone to school with, someone we'd both known growing up.

"He's in the state mental hospital now," she said quietly, her voice weighted with sorrow.

"I've just been holding him in my heart," she said. "It helps me feel close to him. Like maybe it matters somehow."

I paused before responding, deeply moved by the care in her voice.

"I think that's what prayer is," I said slowly. "At least for me. Holding someone in your heart like that is a spiritual act. You're not holding him alone. In my language of faith, God is part of that connection. God is the presence that carries your love across the distance. It *matters* that you love him. It *matters* that you're holding him in your heart."

It was such a simple, yet transformative, relational moment. Each of us was trying to give language to something deeply tender and vulnerable. I didn't need to translate her language into mine or soften my faith to match hers. In that mutual honoring, the threads of connection between us grew stronger, regardless of our differing beliefs.

In moments like these, I believe God is always at work, consecrating the space between us. Love doesn't require shared belief to be present.

On another long walk, Missy told me how she feels in church: "It feels like a cult," she said half-laughing, half-cringing.

"I get that," I said, laughing with her. "Honestly, if I hadn't grown up in the church, I'd probably feel the same way. It's weird, all the standing, sitting, and singing."

We walked on in silence for a while, our footsteps finding an easy rhythm. Me, a Jesus-loving psychologist of religion. Her, a deeply empathetic, nature-bathing atheist. Talking about love and presence and what it means to feel held.

Neither of us needed to defend our ground. We were simply curious, open, and unguarded with each other. Trust was at work between us, not only in the space we shared but *within* each of us.

LOVE DOESN'T REQUIRE SHARED BELIEF TO BE PRESENT.

We each trusted our own grounding enough to stay open to the other. And because of that, the friendship deepened. We didn't need to erase our differences; we could both bring our full selves into the space between us.

What feels simple now would have been nearly impossible for me earlier in life. As a young teenager, I would have tried to please Missy, setting aside my own beliefs in order to stay connected. In my twenties, I might have gone the other direction and tried to convince her, needing her to see the world the same way I did.

But over time, I've learned something different. I've learned that I can stay with myself *and* stay with her.

This kind of unguarded presence is nearly impossible apart from a secure soul.

When we feel unanchored inside, we tend to respond to difference in predictable ways. We either lose ourselves in relationship through pleasing, performing, or shrinking to preserve connection; or we try to manage the other person by working to change, persuade, or control them so we don't have to feel the discomfort of disagreement or differences.

Maybe you recognize some version of these patterns too.

You might find yourself abandoning parts of yourself in order to belong. For example, you might soften your convictions, adapt your language, or stay quiet out of the fear of losing connection.

Or you might notice a different pull altogether. Perhaps you feel compelled to explain, persuade, or correct, especially when something you care about is misunderstood. Even when no one has asked for your opinion, there can be an urgency to be heard, a need for others to see the world the way you do.

These instincts are understandable. They're often attempts to protect connection. But when they're driven by fear rather than love, they can pull us away from ourselves and away from the real connections we desire.

But over time, something shifts. As you learn to care for the different parts of you—recognizing them and returning again and again to God's steady presence—you become more deeply rooted within your own soul. And from that rootedness, a new capacity emerges.

You begin to realize that your beliefs don't require agreement in order to be real. Your viewpoint doesn't need to be defended in every conversation. You can hold your convictions with humility rather than urgency.

And when you're no longer fighting for your footing, curiosity can take the place of fear.

You can listen without preparing a rebuttal.

You can ask questions without feeling threatened by the answers.

You can disagree with someone's ideas while still honoring their humanity.

This is what secure souls look like when they're connected:

- Staying present without controlling
- Honoring difference without collapsing into sameness
- Holding your own convictions without needing someone else to echo them

And when even our most secure relationships falter, when differences grow, words fall short, or healing doesn't happen in the ways we hoped, there is still another way God holds us together in connection, one that does not require proximity, agreement, or resolution.

THE CIRCLE OF CONNECTION

Sometimes, in a moment of clarity—a sudden flash of insight, a burden lifting, or a quiet sense of being held—I pause and wonder: *Who is praying for me right now?*

Is it a friend who knows exactly what I'm going through?

Is it someone from long ago, who simply thought of me with love, and prayed?

Is it my mom?

My mom is a sanctuary of stained glass: intricate, complex, and deeply empathetic. When my mom prays for me, *I feel it.*

Even now, some mornings, when we haven't seen each other for a while, something will spark inside me. A heavy mood will lift. A new thought will break through. I'll feel a sense of being loved.

And I will look at the clock to confirm what I already know. My mom's at Mass praying for me. I feel it in my bones—a thread of warmth and light stretching across the distance.

In that moment, we are connected, held within the same fabric of Love, woven together through prayer.

Prayer is a silent, invisible attachment tether, a way of staying connected across time and space. It's a way of staying *present—of attuning*—to one another in the spiritual realm. It's so much more than speaking to God. It's joining with God, who is already there with you, and with the other person.

Through prayer, you can stay present with someone spiritually, even when you cannot reach them with your body. You can offer words that you're not quite sure how to land face-to-face.

You can bear witness to their ache and entrust them to Love's care.

You can hold them with mercy, even as you maintain a healthy distance.

You can name a frailty, a fear, or a wound without needing to fix, to win, or to prove.

You can also turn prayer inward. You can join with God in staying present to a part of yourself in need, whether it's the Inner Controller who cannot stop striving, the Shadow who keeps shutting down, or the Young One in need of loving presence. You can ask God for the grace to remain patient, discerning, and present within your own inner world.

This is the quiet work of prayer: staying present to what is while trusting Love to do what you cannot.

It's not a one-way line, but a living circle of connection. As you turn toward God, you are held. As you hold another in prayer, they are held. And somehow, you are both nourished by the same Love.

And over time, you begin to notice the fruit of that sacred circle in both profound and ordinary ways. It shows up as a flicker of empathy for a stranger, laughter that softens the edges of a strained relationship, or an unexpected kindness that loosens what once felt stuck.

This is the fruit of a secure soul: trust that holds its center while widening its reach. Love that stays present, even when words fail. Faith that divine Love keeps flowing patiently and faithfully through it all.

Recognize: *I'm scared to trust.*

Return: *I am loved, even here.*

CHAPTER 14

TRUST A CHILD SHALL LEAD

By now, you've met the many parts of your inner world. You've met the Controller, who has tried to hold everything together; the Shadow, who has worked so hard to hide the ache; and the Young One, who never stopped knowing that Love could heal you.

You've walked with them through loneliness, honesty, and moments of real grace. You've watched as each one began to open, to trust, and to take the hand of Love.

And somewhere along the way, you may have noticed a subtle shift inside, a sense that the story of your soul isn't just about these parts anymore, though they'll always be with you. It's about the *wholeness* that begins to form when Love is allowed to weave every one of them together.

It's not that these parts of your soul go away—you

wouldn't want them to. They bring you life and vitality, curiosity and play. They're good inner company.

But over time, the melody of your soul grows richer, more harmonious, more consistently held. The parts within begin to rest more easily. They begin to *trust* more easily. They no longer have to fight for control or prove their worth.

They begin to find their rhythm, again and again, in Love.

That's where I found myself one afternoon, once again walking down the streets of London.

WHEN LOVE WALKS WITH YOU

It's sunny outside, and I am walking down Oxford Street toward Hyde Park, on the other side of Kensington Palace.

Everything I see is magical. Every corner holds some image from a beloved book or movie. Diagon Alley from Harry Potter. The place where Frances Hodgson Burnett wrote *A Little Princess*. Covent Garden, where the girls from Noel Streatfeild's Shoe Books would go to perform. And of course, there's Paddington Station.

I give myself over to the sights, the energy, the enchantment all around me. But then I begin to notice something else. I sense a kind of urgency inside of me, an overwhelming pull to share this moment with somebody.

Nobody sees me!

Nobody knows I'm here!

I am confused by this feeling. It's familiar in the sense that I often notice this feeling on the cusp of any big event or activity or meaningful experience. It's as if I'm chronically alone in my life, with no one to witness it.

It's also distracting. And honestly, a little annoying. It takes me out of the moment. Like, Am I supposed to pick up the phone and call somebody? I don't even think that's possible given the time differences internationally. Am I supposed to post about it right now on social media? I don't actually want to do that. And honestly, it's not what this feeling seems to be about.

Most of me wants to be fully present to *this* moment, the one happening right here in London.

My Inner Controller tries to refocus me.

Just enjoy the walk! Why do you need to tell somebody?

But her efforts don't work. Something inside me needs my attention.

And then I have an epiphany. It's so clear that I stop walking for a moment and almost get rear-ended by the person walking behind me.

This feeling of "Nobody sees me" is coming from the Young One.

I'm curious now, sensing the invitation.

I'm here with you, I let this part of me know gently, this place that feels so alone inside.

Almost instantly, something softens. Aware of my attention, she stops tugging at me—and immediately crawls up on my shoulders to get a better view. *Do you see it? Do you see how amazing this all is?*

The feeling of being unseen is gone. She doesn't need the whole world to notice. She just wants *me* to see what she sees and to unabashedly share this with her.

This moment feels so important, yet so delicate—like when someone you love is finally opening up their heart, and you are scared to move a muscle in case it distracts them.

So I stay still. I assure her that I'm carefully noticing everything she sees. I am *with her.*

A jolt of love for this young girl flows through me. *I'm so grateful you're here with me.*

We are connected and brimming over with the fullness of the moment. That urge to tell somebody else has vanished. I don't need to externalize it. I am delighted to be here with this Young One, and she is over the moon to be here with me.

I am intimately connected *within* my own self. The part of me that has felt so alone, so unseen, is now held. She is fully connected. We are together, even as we are distinct.

But that's not the end of it.

Recognizing what feels like a sacred moment, I find myself wondering if God is near.

And with that single thought—God is here.

Right here, on a random street in London.

I am no longer just me. We are three—a trio:

This Young One filled with awe and wonder.

Me, my adult self, awake and connected.

And God.

God is right here with us, weaving us together with invisible threads of love, behind us and before us and through us.

We are together, and we are also distinct, as we make our way down this street in London.

I have never felt so seen. So connected. So full.

All by myself.

We are many, and we are one; distinct, yet woven together by Love. It's the closest thing to bliss I've ever felt.

Over time, my soul has learned *to return to that kind of Love*—again and again and again.

Here's what I know to be true:

Love will keep finding you.

Again and again and again.

Parts of you will drift, strive, or retreat.

And when you notice—just breathe.

Because God is already here.

Each time you *recognize* disconnection and *return* to Love, trust grows—

within you,

between you and God,

between you and others.

And over time, you become a safe place for the tender parts of your own soul, and for the people you love.

A soul held. A soul steadied. A soul made secure by Love.

Recognize: *The Young One will lead the way.*

Return: *I am beloved.*

ACKNOWLEDGMENTS

It's new for me to write so personally. It feels uncomfortable, and a little vulnerable. I want to begin by thanking Lisa-Jo Baker, who invited me to step out from behind the "expert" role and tell more of my own story. Thank you—not only for that invitation, but for staying so present with me throughout these pages by modeling both compassion and containment. And for letting your mastery of the art of writing, and your thoughtful wisdom, guide me and so many others.

I also want to acknowledge my first and dearest attachment figures. To Mom, Dad, and Court—each of you has given me a different kind of gift, and I carry them all within me. Together, your big hearts, deep-belly laughs, and generosity of spirit have been rich soil for my life, helping me grow, take root, and expand. And to my beloved grandparents, Bomma and Boppa—though you are no longer here, the love you gave me remains. I'm so grateful.

To my husband, Joe—thank you for seeing me and for showing me, again and again, what safety feels like. And to

Brooke, Chase, and Maddy, thank you for being the world's best family and for making the emptying of the nest a little less like loss and a little more like love expanding.

To my friend Missy—thank you for the long arc of your friendship, for knowing me then and loving me now, and for letting me share our story in these pages. And to Kate, thank you for believing in me so consistently—for encouraging me to share my story, and for staying with me every step of the way. To Rachel Jacobson, thank you for your steadiness and thoughtful care. And to the entire W team, Lisa-Jo, Damon, Caren, Allison, Brooke, Lauren, and the whole crew working behind the scenes—thank you for your incredible skill, your care, and your belief in this work. I'm grateful for every one of you. Lastly, to Heather, Jonni, Kelly, and Giulia: What a gift it is to do this work alongside women who are brilliant, generous, and deeply good at what they do.

And finally, to the God who stays—the One who has met me in ways I once thought impossible—thank you. Thank you for this gift of creating. For filling in the gaps when words fall short. For being present in every ache, every striving, every hidden place—and for so faithfully gathering every part of me back into Love.

NOTES

CHAPTER 1

1. See Daniel J. Siegel and Tina Payne Bryson, *The Power of Showing Up: How Parental Presence Shapes Who Our Kids Become and How Their Brains Get Wired* (Ballantine Books, 2020); Curt Thompson, *Anatomy of the Soul: Surprising Connections Between Neuroscience and Spiritual Practices That Can Transform Your Life and Relationships* (Tyndale Momentum, 2010).
2. The concept of "secure attachment" comes from the work of John Bowlby and Mary Ainsworth, whose research established the patterns of attachment widely used in psychology today. See John Bowlby, *Attachment*, Attachment and Loss, vol. 1, 2nd ed. (Basic Books, 1982); Mary D. Salter Ainsworth et al., *Patterns of Attachment: A Psychological Study of the Strange Situation* (Psychology Press, 1978).
3. Bowlby's early writings describe attachment behavior as biologically rooted proximity-seeking that supports safety and survival and becomes a foundation for later expectations about care and security. See Bowlby, Attachment and Loss.
4. Attachment theory does describe "internal working models" that shape expectations of safety and care, but it doesn't typically provide the parts-based language many readers

find helpful for naming internal voices and roles. For a parts-based model, see Richard C. Schwartz and Martha Sweezy, *Internal Family Systems Therapy*, 2nd ed. (Guilford Press, 2019); Richard C. Schwartz, *No Bad Parts: Healing Trauma and Restoring Wholeness with the Internal Family Systems Model* (Sounds True, 2021).

5. In this book, I'm integrating attachment theory, parts language, and Christian contemplative theology into a formation framework. While my work has been informed by insights from Internal Family Systems (IFS), this is not a presentation of the IFS clinical model. For a Christian adaptation of the IFS model in a practical therapeutic framework, see Alison Cook and Kimberly Miller, *Boundaries for Your Soul: How to Turn Your Overwhelming Thoughts and Feelings into Your Greatest Allies* (Thomas Nelson, 2018).
6. Lisa Miller's work highlights the human capacity for spiritual awareness and suggests that spirituality is not a niche personality trait but an innate dimension of human life with measurable correlates in the brain. See Lisa Miller, *The Awakened Brain: The New Science of Spirituality and Our Quest for an Inspired Life* (Random House, 2021).
7. For a beautiful resource on this inner garden as a living ecosystem, see Dr. Anita Phillips, *The Garden Within: Where the War with Your Emotions Ends and Your Most Powerful Life Begins* (Nelson Books, 2023).
8. I appreciate John Eldredge's use of the phrase "young place" as a way of naming the tender, earlier parts of us that still carry longing and pain. See John Eldredge, *Experience Jesus. Really: Finding Refuge, Strength, and Wonder through Everyday Encounters with God* (Nelson Books, 2025), 137.
9. Irvin Yalom's work has been formative for me in naming isolation as a central human struggle—one that therapy can illuminate but that also points us toward deeper questions of meaning, presence, and belonging. See Irvin D. Yalom, *Existential Psychotherapy* (Basic Books, 1980), 355.

10. Walter Bauer et al., *A Greek-English Lexicon of the New Testament and Other Early Christian Literature*, 3rd ed. (University of Chicago Press, 2000), under "σῴζω."

CHAPTER 2

1. This study is often cited for its early contribution to our understanding that social exclusion is not just emotionally painful—it can engage neural circuitry associated with distress and pain processing. Naomi I. Eisenberger et al., "Does Rejection Hurt? An fMRI Study of Social Exclusion," *Science* 302, no. 5643 (2003): 290–292, https://doi.org/10.1126/science.1089134.
2. Chuck DeGroat offers a wise, compassionate guide for tending to the inner life—especially for those carrying spiritual wounds, exhaustion, or a sense of fragmentation. See Chuck DeGroat, *Healing What's Within: Coming Home to Yourself—and to God—When You're Wounded, Weary & Wandering* (Tyndale Refresh, 2024).

CHAPTER 3

1. I adapted this phrasing from Sue Monk Kidd's novel *The Book of Longings* (Penguin Books, 2020), 13.
2. I love how Emily P. Freeman gives language for the wisdom of staying *and* the courage of leaving. Emily P. Freeman, *How to Walk into a Room: The Art of Knowing When to Stay and When to Walk Away* (HarperOne, 2024).
3. John M. Gottman and Joan DeClaire, *The Relationship Cure: A 5 Step Guide to Strengthening Your Marriage, Family, and Friendships* (Random House, 2002), 4.
4. My understanding of "parts" is informed by Dr. Richard Schwartz and the Internal Family Systems (IFS) model, which describes three broad categories of parts—managers, firefighters, and exiles. In this book, however, I develop a simplified and spiritually integrated template of three parts that reflects my own observations and theological commitments.
5. See Bessel van der Kolk, *The Body Keeps the Score: Brain,*

Mind, and Body in the Healing of Trauma (Penguin Books, 2014), which affirms the multifaceted nature of the human self and the integration required for healing.

6. This language is adapted from Henri J. M. Nouwen's writings on solitude and the inner life and from my earlier synthesis of these themes in my book *Boundaries for Your Soul*. See Henri J. M. Nouwen, *The Way of the Heart: Desert Spirituality and Contemporary Ministry* (Seabury Press, 1981); Alison Cook and Kimberly Miller, *Boundaries for Your Soul: How to Turn Your Overwhelming Thoughts and Feelings into Your Greatest Allies* (Thomas Nelson, 2018).
7. My previous work has explored the "true self" not as self-perfection, but as the grounded, honest place from which we can live and love more freely. See Alison Cook, *The Best of You: Break Free from Painful Patterns, Mend Your Past, and Discover Your True Self in God* (Nelson Books, 2022).
8. Daniel J. Siegel, *Mindsight: The New Science of Personal Transformation* (Bantam Books, 2010), 44–45, Kindle.

CHAPTER 4

1. Daniel J. Siegel, *Mindsight: The New Science of Personal Transformation* (Bantam Books, 2010), 312, Kindle.
2. For an accessible introduction to the nervous system's cues of safety and threat (polyvagal theory) and practical ways to work with it, see Deb Dana, *Anchored: How to Befriend Your Nervous System Using Polyvagal Theory* (Sounds True, 2021); and Stephen W. Porges, *The Polyvagal Theory: Neurophysiological Foundations of Emotions, Attachment, Communication, and Self-Regulation* (W. W. Norton, 2011).
3. I am drawing on anxious/avoidant attachment styles here. For two helpful resources on attachment styles, see Amir Levine and Rachel S. F. Heller, *Attached: The New Science of Adult Attachment and How It Can Help You Find—and Keep—Love* (TarcherPerigee, 2010); and Nedra Glover Tawwab, *The Balancing Act: Creating Healthy Dependency and Connection Without Losing Yourself* (Tarcher, 2026).

CHAPTER 5

1. Augustine and Aquinas described sin as a disordered love, and Ann Voskamp's use of this idea in *WayMaker* prompted me to revisit this theological tradition and its relevance to longing, attachment, and the inner life. See Augustine, *The City of God against the Pagans*, ed. and trans. R. W. Dyson (Cambridge University Press, 1998), book 15, chapter 22; Thomas Aquinas, *Summa Theologica*, trans. Fathers of the English Dominican Province, part I–II (Benziger Bros., 1947), question 84, article 1; and Ann Voskamp, *WayMaker: Finding the Way to the Life You've Always Dreamed Of* (W Publishing Group, 2022).
2. Henri J. M. Nouwen, *The Wounded Healer: Ministry in Contemporary Society* (Image, 1979).
3. Chuck DeGroat, *Healing What's Within: Coming Home to Yourself—and to God—When You're Wounded, Weary & Wandering* (Tyndale Refresh, 2024), 140.
4. Curt Thompson, *The Soul of Shame: Retelling the Stories We Believe About Ourselves* (IVP Books, 2015).
5. Hillary L. McBride, *The Wisdom of Your Body: Finding Healing, Wholeness, and Connection through Embodied Living* (Brazos Press, 2021).

CHAPTER 6

1. Richard C. Schwartz, *Internal Family Systems Therapy* (Guilford Press, 1995), 42.

CHAPTER 7

1. The Young One, as I'm using it here, draws from multiple streams: what Internal Family Systems (IFS) calls an exile; the inner child tradition—the developmentally young place where attachment wounds first come into conscious awareness; and the Christian contemplative stream that honors the child as a bearer of spiritual perception and wisdom.
2. Daniel J. Siegel, *Mindsight: The New Science of Personal Transformation* (Bantam Books, 2010), 66.
3. Alice Miller, *The Drama of the Gifted Child: The Search*

for the True Self, trans. Ruth Ward, rev. ed. (Basic Books, 1997).

4. My understanding of childlike trust has been informed by numerous authors, especially Richard Rohr, *Falling Upward: A Spirituality for the Two Halves of Life* (Jossey-Bass, 2011); and David G. Benner, *Surrender to Love: Discovering the Heart of Christian Spirituality* (IVP Books, 2003).

CHAPTER 8

1. See Lisa Miller, *The Awakened Brain: The New Science of Spirituality and Our Quest for an Inspired Life* (Random House, 2021), 9–10.
2. Ana-Maria Rizzuto, *The Birth of the Living God: A Psychoanalytic Study* (University of Chicago Press, 1979), 37.
3. Curt Thompson, *Anatomy of the Soul: Surprising Connections Between Neuroscience and Spiritual Practices That Can Transform Your Life and Relationships* (Tyndale Momentum, 2010), 118.
4. See Lee A. Kirkpatrick, *Attachment, Evolution, and the Psychology of Religion* (Guilford Press, 2005). Kirkpatrick's research demonstrates that individuals' attachment to God often parallels their earliest attachment experiences, shaping how they give and receive love in relationship to the Divine.
5. N. T. Wright, *Surprised by Hope: Rethinking Heaven, the Resurrection, and the Mission of the Church* (HarperOne, 2008).
6. See Aundi Kolber, *Try Softer: A Fresh Approach to Move Us Out of Anxiety, Stress, and Survival Mode—and into a Life of Connection and Joy* (Tyndale Momentum, 2020).
7. John Mayer, "Good Love Is on the Way (Acoustic)," track 4 on *The Village Sessions*, Aware Records, 2006.

CHAPTER 9

1. This section is adapted from my "Name, Frame, Brave" framework for working with painful emotions. See Alison Cook, *I Shouldn't Feel This Way: Name What's Hard,*

Tame Your Guilt, and Transform Self-Sabotage into Brave Action (Nelson Books, 2024).

CHAPTER 10

1. For specific research findings, see Kristin D. Neff et al., "Self-Compassion, Achievement Goals, and Coping with Academic Failure," *Self and Identity* 4, no. 3 (2005): 263–287, https://doi.org/10.1080/13576500444000317; and Kristin D. Neff et al., "Self-Compassion and Adaptive Psychological Functioning," *Journal of Research in Personality* 41, no. 1 (2007): 139–154, https://doi.org/10.1016/j.jrp.2006.03.004. For more accessible reading on self-compassion, see Kristin Neff, *Self-Compassion: The Proven Power of Being Kind to Yourself* (William Morrow, 2011); and Aundi Kolber, *Try Softer: A Fresh Approach to Move Us Out of Anxiety, Stress, and Survival Mode—and into a Life of Connection and Joy* (Tyndale Momentum, 2020).
2. Robert Puff, "The Power of Self-Forgiveness: How to Break Free from the Chains of Past Mistakes," *Psychology Today*, January 13, 2025, https://www.psychologytoday.com/us/blog/meditation-for-modern-life/202501/the-power-of-self-forgiveness.
3. For a beautiful definition of the broken spirit, see Christopher Cook, *Healing What You Can't Erase: Transform Your Mental, Emotional, and Spiritual Health from the Inside Out* (WaterBrook, 2024), 37.

CHAPTER 11

1. I adapted this quote from a phrase posted on Instagram on October 16, 2024, by my friend and fellow therapist Aundi Kolber: "Work from love, not for love."
2. Ps. 62:1, emphasis mine, paraphrased.
3. Two wonderful explanations of the spiritual power of imagination are in C. S. Lewis's *Surprised by Joy: The Shape of My Early Life* (Geoffrey Bles, 1955), and in Michael John Cusick's *Sacred Attachment: Escaping*

Spiritual Exhaustion and Trusting in Divine Love (InterVarsity Press, 2025).

4. Brené Brown's work on vulnerability and wholehearted living has shaped much of my thinking about risk and vulnerability. See Brené Brown, *Daring Greatly: How the Courage to Be Vulnerable Transforms the Way We Live, Love, Parent, and Lead* (New York: Avery, 2015).

CHAPTER 12

1. Wendell Berry, *The Unsettling of America: Culture and Agriculture* (Counterpoint), 2015, Kindle 90.
2. Heart, "Never," track 3 on *Heart*, Capitol Records, 1985.

CHAPTER 13

1. *Friends*, season 3, episode 20, "The One with the Dollhouse," written by Wil Calhoun, directed by Terry Hughes, aired April 10, 1997, on NBC.

ABOUT THE AUTHOR

Dr. Alison Cook is a psychologist of religion, licensed therapist, and host of the top-ranked *The Best of You* podcast. She is the author of several best-selling books, including *Boundaries for Your Soul*. Known for her work at the intersection of faith, psychology, and spiritual formation, she helps people cultivate a secure inner life—healing past wounds, strengthening a grounded sense of self, building healthy relationships, and experiencing God as a steady and loving presence in their lives. She and her husband, Joe, are the parents of two adult children and call both Boston and Wyoming home. Connect with Dr. Alison at www.dralisoncook.com.

Also available by Dr. Alison Cook, wherever books are sold.